David Swing

Truths for Today

Spoken in the Past Winter

David Swing

Truths for Today
Spoken in the Past Winter

ISBN/EAN: 9783337249113

Printed in Europe, USA, Canada, Australia, Japan

Cover: Foto ©Lupo / pixelio.de

More available books at **www.hansebooks.com**

TRUTHS FOR TO-DAY

SPOKEN IN THE PAST WINTER.

BY DAVID SWING,

PASTOR FOURTH PRESBYTERIAN CHURCH.

CHICAGO:

JANSEN, McCLURG AND COMPANY.

1874.

KNIGHT & LEONARD, PRINTERS, CHICAGO.

CONTENTS.

SERMON I.

RELIGIOUS TOLERATION, OR CHARITY.

ROMANS 14 : 1.—Him that is weak in the faith, receive ye, but not to doubtful disputations; for one believeth that he may eat all things; another, who is weak, eateth herbs 11

SERMON II.

THE GOLDEN RULE.

MATTHEW 7 : 12.—Therefore all things whatsoever ye would that men should do to you, do you even so to them; for this is the law and the prophets - - - - - - - 31

SERMON III.

RIGHTEOUSNESS.

PSALMS 48 : 10.—Thy right hand is full of righteousness - 49

SERMON XII.

ST. PAUL - - - - - - 219

SERMON XIII.

FAITH.

John 3 : 36.—He that believeth on the Son hath everlasting life, and he that believeth not the Son shall not see life, but the wrath of God abideth on him - - - 237

SERMON XIV.

ST. JOHN - - - - - - 259

SERMON XV.

IMMORTAL LIFE.

Luke 20 : 38.—For he is not a God of the dead but of the living, for all live unto him - - - - 277

ADDENDA — SECOND EDITION.

SERMON XVI.

A REASONABLE ORTHODOXY.

ROM. 12:1.—Present your bodies a living sacrifice, holy, acceptable unto God, your reasonable service - - - 293

DECLARATION,

In reply to the charges of Prof. Patton - - - - - - 311

RELIGIOUS TOLERATION, OR CHARITY.

SERMON I.

RELIGIOUS TOLERATION, OR CHARITY.

"**Him that is weak in the faith, receive ye, but not to doubtful disputations; for one believeth that he may eat all things; another, who is weak, eateth herbs."**—*Rom. 14: 1.*

YOU may consider this entire chapter to be the source of my theme, and the theme, therefore, to be the *Toleration of Religious Opinion.*

The word "toleration" suffers a change of meaning in successive times. To suffer an opposite sect to worship at all, to suffer your religious opposite to live, was once the meaning of toleration. But we have passed beyond that usage of the term, and have come to a better age, when toleration means the extending toward one of different belief our friendship and all the civilities of refined or Christian life. Not daring any more to put men to death for their opinions, the question remains as to how much ill feeling we must suppress and actual good-will reveal. This is the form assumed by the question in our enlightened and free country.

We suffer this morning the pain that comes from discussing a subject too large for the hour — a subject the complete investigation of which would demand your study, your reading, your deep interest, for days instead of moments. Each week in this era, when the world has grown so broad in its means of investigation and in its power to investigate, the pulpit more and more must feel that it can only suggest lines of thought, and in its half hour indicate subjects worthy of the more deliberate and thorough study of the multitude. In our vast world, the clergy and all public speakers have become only an index of the book of knowledge, instead of being the grand solid volume in which the wisdom is all elaborated. In the ages of great vices the clergy were likened unto finger-boards which pointed out to others paths in which they did not themselves journey. This is perhaps no longer true as to virtue, but it is as to knowledge, for, like finger-boards, we can point out the paths of study and research, but are unable to go with you in the long but impressive journey.

This chapter from St. Paul is worthy of being learned by heart, and then, in many a silent hour when alone, we would find discourses flowing into our souls from that great perennial fountain. The words, him that is weak in the faith receive, but not to doubtful disputations, draw their truthfulness from the very nature and condition of man. The fact that man is by nature imperfect, makes it necessary that he should also be tolerant. The fate that gave man a career of comparative ignorance ought to secure for him a career full of charity and forgiveness given and received. There is nothing more universal than ignorance, and hence there should be no virtue more universal than toleration of religious opinion. By ignorance I do not mean barbarism, but that humility of knowledge confessed by even the most learned of each successive generation. The facility with which we all absorb error, the readiness with which we all fall into deep and blind prejudices, should make us always ready, not indeed to excuse sin against light, but to tolerate many shades of religious opinion. It is folly to demand a unity of belief in a world where there is no one wise but God, and no one good except God. Some of the best men who have ever lived are now seen to have been the victims of great errors; and the persecutions they carried forward in the name of their superior wisdom appear to us now in a bad light indeed, when it is now evident that they themselves held only a very imperfect system of doctrine. Their mistake lay in the assumption that they had reached the ideal in religion; whereas, God only holds the ideal in knowledge; man deals only in the imperfect. It was a maxim of the ancients that you must not praise one until after he is dead, for there is no security that he may not commit a crime or reveal a folly even in his most mature days. The old statesman may at last accept a bribe, or may, having been a republican, become at last an aristocrat and a despot. We must pause until he has ended his career, and then, if he dies in perfect honor, praise may chant its song safely over that tomb which ends all the vicissitudes of earth. Cæsar set out as a great Roman republican, the hater of crowns and lover of the dear people; but, says the play, "Was the crown offered him thrice? Aye, marry, was't, and he put it by thrice, every time gentler than the other." According to history, Cæsar's democracy was being drained out of him in the late years of his career, thus showing us that the grave is the place for pronouncing the true eulogy over man. After God has let the curtain fall, then we can come with our estimate of love or sorrow.

The same philosophy must apply to the forms of Christianity that walk in a sort of individual life before us. I should not be willing to put to death any one for not being a Presbyterian or a Methodist, not be willing because these religions have not come to their final estimate. There may be great errors within them that have escaped our sight, some hidden evil, like that in Cæsar, which made him push back the crown each time gentler than before. It is possible that some other form of doctrine might have brought greater virtue and happiness to society, and it is possible that out of the future a church will be born dearer than either both to man and God. Hence it is necessary for those living within these two vast denominations to move along in charity toward mankind, waiting not for the tomb, in this case, for they may not perish, but for the verdict of futurity. If in the end of the human race, or in the end of this or the next century, the millions of earth shall look back and say that Presbyterianism or Methodism led a useful, beautiful life, and then sweetly died because of something better, that praise will sound like music over our tombs, unsullied either by egotism or blood. The Savior said, "Why call ye me good? there is none good but God." None wise but Him. Hence the highest aspiration of an individual or a church should be to walk along in humility and tenderness, and wait for the final verdict of God and humanity.

All intolerance is based upon egotism. It proceeds

from the assumption that you have reached the ideal. When the Puritans banished the Quakers it was done upon the assumption that the Pilgrims had brought the ideal over in their ship. They confessed themselves to represent God in doctrine and sentiment. But now that a few centuries have passed, and we are permitted to see the Puritan and the Quaker in the light of long generations, we perceive that the most truth and the best truth was in the keeping, not of those who ordained the banishment, but of those who endured it. The dreadful persecution to which the Catholics subjected the world all originated in a *human egotism* that cried, "I have found it! I have found it!" They had become the exponents of God. Whereas now history shows that in all cases the persons exiled or put to death held a better creed at the time than those who forced upon them the bitter fate. The origin of intolerance has never been the deeper truth but the deeper egotism. It comes from a forgetfulness that God only is wise, and from an assumed agency for the Almighty in worldly affairs.

It is a weakness of man that when, in business affairs, he is employed to perform some office for an estate or a government or corporation, he by some strange metamorphosis, not mentioned in Ovid, becomes very soon the owner of the estate or the center and soul of the government, or sole owner of the caravansera or the empire. .Intolerance in religion is nothing else than the outcropping of this human infirmity amid other surroundings. All the difference is that this graver assumption possesses an egotism more solemn and less manifest; but it is the same self-transformation of a mortal into a Deity. It is a proverb of the Bible, "Let not him that girdeth on his armor boast himself as he that taketh it off," for the events that may come on between the morning of the battle and its night are many and unreadable. The heart, however strong and confident, must wait till the struggle is over. This rule must be seen at once to apply to all individual and sectarian life. In a world of uncertainty, that applies to the realm of truth as well as to that of military skill, one dare not boast until the warfare is over. Each one must pursue his path of duty with fidelity, and then calmly wait for time or eternity to measure the quality and quantity of the truth and the service. It ought to be a warning against all feeling of intolerance that the ideas over which most blood has been shed, have in subsequent experience and thought, been proven to be either useless or false. The dogmas for which one age has put thousands to death, have by a subsequent age been withdrawn as false, or neglected because

2

useless. But one might have premised that the most intolerance would always be found gathered about the least valuable doctrine, because the most valuable doctrines are always so evident to human reason that no thumb-screw or faggot is ever needed to make the lips whisper assent. Over the idea that two and two make four no blood has been shed; but over the insinuation that three may be one, or one three, there has often been a demand for external influence to brace up for the work the frail logical faculty. It is probable that no man has ever been put to death for heresy regarding the Sermon on the Mount. Its declarations demand no tortures to aid human faith; but when a church comes along with its "legitimacy," or with its Five Points, or with its Prayer Book, or its Infant Baptism, or Eternal Procession of the Holy Ghost, then comes the demand for the rack and the stake to make up in terrorism what is wanting in evidence. In the fourth century Christianity had already been divided up into ninety different sects. Whether Christ had two souls, one human and the other Divine, became a dividing question, and each party persecuted the other. And, also, the time of celebrating Easter involved the salvation or damnation of men. And when the nature of the light at the Transfiguration was discussed, at an early council, it was resolved that anyone contending that the light making the halo about Christ was not uncreated — a soul brilliancy — should be deprived of Christian burial at life's close. Thus, where evidence was most wanting, it has been most customary to find outside aids to faith. When witnesses were wanting, the High Priests rent their clothes.

History will, no doubt, bear me out in the assertion that the quantity of intolerance has always been inversely as the value of the doctrine, the greatest bigotry always crystallizing around the least valuable idea. If God has so fashioned the human mind that all its myriad forms can agree upon doctrines that are most vital; and if, as a fact, persecution has always attached itself to the small, then we would seem to have the curse of God visibly revealed against intolerance, in the fact that He has separated it from the large and evident, and linked its destiny to that which is both unimportant and doubtful. With the experience and exposures of a thousand years before us, we all, if feelings of intolerance rise in our hearts, are bound to feel that, perhaps, we have fallen down from the upper air, and are lying flat in that realm of non-essentials, whose support has always come, not from sweet truth, but from passion.

If you say, have not all the sects an inspired guide in the New Testament? Can they not all read the same words, and thus reproduce the same church and the same creed? The answer is easy: An inspired word does not insure an inspired interpretation. The marriage contract is an inspired institution, perhaps. Assume it to be such. The details of its rights and powers are human. It is a divine union, subjected to human rendering. In order to make the marriage relation perfect, all possible forms and circumstances of it should have been furnished men along with the central idea. But the creator never perfectly equips man. He gives him a feeble outfit, like a son started by his father for a new country. The son has a common school education, habits of industry, and a hundred pounds. Subsequent things must come by subsequent labor. The Bible gives only an outfit — the implements of industry. The Bible is thus submitted to human interpretation; and thus inspiration, like the river through old Eden, is divided up into four parts. The Presbyterian reads *Preacher;* the Episcopalian takes up the same page and reads *Bishop;* the Calvinist sees all the words that exalt fate; the Arminian all the words that exalt free will; in baptism, the Baptists behold a man applied to water, the other sects behold water applied to the man. It is thus readily seen that inspiration will not secure unity unless there be inspired interpretation, and then interpretation of that version, onward and onward, until the mind of man is wholly superseded by the infinite interference of God. An Episcopalian clergyman once said in my hearing, that when Paul sent for the garment he left at Troas, what he wanted was the surplice used in his sacred oratory; whereas other denominations suppose it was the grand old Roman cloak, worn not so much in the name of religion, as in the name of the North Wind. Either theory is adequate, for there is no doubt the classic speakers used their cloak as a part of rhetoric, and there is no doubt it was valuable, all through the damp winter solstice. Inspiration, therefore, does not promise unity of belief. So the Bible speaks of witchcraft and of lunacy; but it does not inform mankind how to discriminate between the witch and the lunatic. Hence, whereas our ancestors hung ten thousand witches, we build asylums for ten thousand insane, and protect with love, perhaps, those whom a former age consumed with fire.

The fact of a Bible will not secure unity of belief and action, because in the interpretation the human mind reappears in all its individuality and lawlessness. No truth can be so plainly set forth that subsequent generations will not stumble amid the words and sentences of the place that uttered them. No men are more accustomed than lawyers and lawmakers to an exact use of words, but it used to be said that American law, once gathered up, had to be sent to England to be interpreted for the very nation that made it; and for this reason the interpretation of law is the chief pursuit of the very mind that expresses and enacts it. In such a world unity of religious belief could only be secured by God's silencing the human mind, and placing himself upon the throne of human reason, with reason bound in chains at his feet. But this would be the annihilation of man, and better than this is the progress of man, with a charity as broad as human life; with a toleration as universal as our ignorance and our mistakes; with a mutual forgiveness as omnipresent as are the shadows and mysteries of human life. All that is needed is a diversity without sorrow or even surprise, a variety as of clouds or wild-flowers.

We stated, a few moments since, that it is the tendency and necessity of intolerance to spend its force upon the least significant doctrines that spring from authority or fancy rather than from the most evident wants of society. To determine what doctrines are essential, and to feel how misplaced all intolerance has been, just look back, and you will see how few are the valuable ideas that emerge from a given age and reveal themselves. Oh, is it possible that the thousands of tenets for which men were racked were too feeble to outlive the very fire that burnt the heretic! Oh, yes, it is possible! Heretic and fire and the idea are all gone together. The idea that killed noble men was itself too feeble to live.

Look back over the history of Jewish or Catholic or Waldensian or Protestant sect, and when you seek for their ideas of value you come at last to their charity and purity and faith in God and the Savior—their pursuit of knowledge and hope of heaven. You think of nothing else. You shovel away the dust and débris of centuries, that by chance you may come upon these jewels in the diadem of religion. And if you find these, you bless the old Church that lived and died on the spot. But all else is beneath your notice. Rubric, surplice, prayer book, two souls of Christ, the Easter time, the transfiguration light, the election, the predestination, the laying on of hands, all count no more with the thoughtful historian seeking for the merits of an age than counted the costumes of those eras or the carriages they drove. We place them below price. There is a certain divine instinct in man that enables him when measuring the past to become noble, and seize upon the valuable elements in character, and pass by the temporary without any doubt or regret; but dealing with the present, this divine instinct seems to. desert us, and, grasping an accident in our arms, we permit virtue and faith and charity, God and heaven, to fall through to the dust. How is it that when we contemplate either the past or the future a certain nobleness goes with us that overlooks all small things and cleaves to the good, and that all the littleness we possess is concentrated within the pulse-beats of to-day? The only explanation must be this — that each man's real life is smaller than his soul. It is belittled by the prejudices and interests of the passing hour; but when he goes to examine the past, or throws his mind forward a century, he leaves behind him his sect and his ambition and his outlook of business and his real estate, and goes to the past and the future only as a soul, a thing of thought and love, an image of the Almighty. We love the simplicity of our fathers who were virtuous, in plain houses; looking to the future, we see a return to simplicity and call it a golden age, but in the present we love furniture and to fare sumptuously every day. This is because the present grinds us by its customs and sins, and hence escaping backward or forward we behold the truth as it is in God. Thus the soul of each man is greater always than his daily life. Present business and vices eclipse the spirit.

In order, therefore, to find the best idea of the Christian Church, and perfectly to escape the intolerant spirit, one would do well to resort to the past, where he can perceive that the ideas over which most blood was shed were ideas that died soonest, and that were of least utility while living; or would do well to rush to the future and there find that only a few cardinal truths of character and of the cross, of virtue and heaven, have dared to assemble in the holy air. Backward or forward, and there is seen a wonderful death of the small and wonderful resurrection of the great, because, backward or forward either, there is a wonderful return of the soul to the justice and intuition of its Maker. Reflection, backward or forward, is like that strange mirage along the lakes whereby cities and landscapes are repeated in the sky in only their purity, all their sins, and diseases, and miasmas, and crimes, and sorrows, being left on the ground beneath. The outlines of palaces, the spires of God's temples, the forests, the everlasting hills, are the only things worthy of being uplifted by the white arms of the radiant light. So in history, or in futurity, we see the Christian Church in the sublime outline of Jesus Christ, all else being left in the dust beneath.

Having in this brief argument found a ground for religious toleration in the natural uncertainty of human knowledge, and in the fact that men have persecuted their fellows most over the smallest ideas, I would say only a few words against any form of intolerance, even when confessed errors exist in their worst possible forms. Suppose the heretic, as the world calls him, pronounces Christ an impostor, and denies the existence of God, still all the light that will ever come into his mind from man will be along the chords of friendship passing from the better heart to his. Words spoken without bitterness, spoken with the confession full and free of human equality, words wreathed with friendship, are the only ones that ever penetrate the soul. The man who hates us, and whom we hate, need not speak. His words are like a discord. Thus the ill-will of the old Puritans jarred like bells jangled out of tune upon the ear of Thomas Paine, and each anathema from the Church only separated him farther from the presence and beauty of God, for God is not a God of discord, but of harmony. One of the ancient Greeks perceived this means of converting men, when he said "the boxer advances with a closed fist, but the orator always with an open hand."

God has so created his human children that all their best happiness, their best home, their best government, their best reform, their best literature, their best art, springs up from a deep friendship from man to man. Thus, therefore, the best Christianity will come, come the most, and the most rapidly. God himself being happiness and love, and the blessed Savior having come to earth in the name of an infinite friendship, the genius and destiny of earth are mirrored in the Creator and Savior, and earth's reform will come like republicanism and the arts, not by the discord of souls, but by their loving brotherhood. Friendship is the condition of civilization.

The classics used to call all the studies of scholars—history, poetry, art, eloquence, music—the humanities, because they brought no wars, no bloodshed, but set out from a human love and advanced in the name of pleasure and peace.

Shall we not open the sacred list and insert among the dear humanities that religion, whose love surpasses all measurement, and whose tears for man fall like dew from the manger to the cross? The first disciples came not by violence, but by a blessed invitation. One of them was grandly transformed, not by persecution, but by resting in peace where his head was near a divine heart. In the name of such a sublime scene we are all bound to speak religion's truths in love, and to offer our fellow men, not doubtful disputations, but a place of forgiveness and peace upon a heart divine in breadth and tenderness.

THE GOLDEN RULE.

SERMON II.

THE GOLDEN RULE.

"Therefore all things whatsoever ye would that men should do to you, do you even so to them; for this is the law and the prophets."—*Matt. 7 : 12.*

THE transition from barbarous to civilized life may be read by the progress made toward just and uniform and universal laws. If the quantity of gold were an evidence of civilization, the Spaniards of old Mexico equaled New England in the civilized condition. If raiment and elegant furniture and palaces were a proof of human progress, the Turks and the Chinese emperors have long been the equals of Washington and Lincoln. But it seems evident that, in the composition of the Mexican, and Turk, and Orientalist at large, there is some element wanting, preventing their condition from being a culture, a civilization. While it is impossible to find all the delicate threads that make up a great and complete human character, it seems evident that no one fact so truly indicates civilization as the presence and activity in a nation of general laws of right, and industry, and happiness — wise, and tender, and uniform. The libraries of England, her myriad ships, her literature, would not complete for her a form of civilization, if she still held slaves, or still hung children for theft, or hung old women for witchcraft, that is, for dressing in black and growing weak in body and mind. And America was the reproach of the family of nations until she freed her slaves. The highest idea man can cherish being that of right, and the most divine conduct being obedience to the laws of right, there could be no high civilization with such an idea and such a conduct disregarded; and hence the honor of civilization never comes with man's furniture, and silks, and gold, and commerce, but with his broad, intelligent justice. It being so essential, therefore, that each individual be engaged in the practice of justice, and that each member of society receive a fair treatment from all around him, a law expressed in words that shall be brief, true, and easily comprehended, is more desirable than pages of philosophy or of poetry, or galleries of art.

The golden rule is no doubt one of the most fundamental laws that can ever be expressed in words or carried in the mind of man. Nature's great law, that matter attracts matter, that a vast central world will attract planets from a straight line into a circle, that an earth will draw a falling apple to itself, and hold its liquid sea and liquid air close to itself, and will hold the seas under the air and the land under the sea, is not more fundamental in the material world than the golden rule is in the world of duty and happiness. Take away the single principle discovered by Newton, and the organized universe is at once dissolved, air and water and land mingle, our globe would become a fluid, and fill its orbit with a floating débris of itself. The golden rule underlies our public and private justice, our society, our charity, our education, our religion; and the sorrows of bad government, of famine, of war, of caste, of slavery, have come from contempt of this principle.

Of the origin of this statement little can be learned. It is almost impossible to conceive of any degree of enlightenment that could have escaped it; it would seem so easy for any one seeing a fellow-man committing an unjust and cruel act to say, "How would you like to be treated in that style?" And yet whenever such a feeling of inquiry has risen in the heart that has been the shadow of the golden rule —the question, How would you love to be treated thus? is the principle. It is difficult to imagine a day that could have been ignorant of this application of justice. It must have been the lament of Cain over the dead body of Abel, that he had done as he would not have wished to be done by. It is incredible that any historic land should wholly have escaped the thought. The history of the world is so imperfect, and then so far as it goes is only a history of wars and kings, and not a history at all of morals or thought, that we know little of the maxims and constitutions that lay beneath old actions. What David thought after he had slain Uriah, or what Cæsar thought when he had murdered a few hundred thousand Germans, can never be culled from a history that looked with contempt upon any facts less conspicuous than a crown or a pageant, or a battle-field. Even if over the most of the great heathen world there rolled such a cloud of vice and cruelty that the public never came up to this sweet sense of reciprocal kindness, yet there might have been tender hearts here and there in all ages, from Babylon and Tyre to Rome and Athens, that wept tears of sympathy in the name of the golden rule. In Confucius, at last, this divine instinct of the soul began to break forth in history. He said, "You must not do to others what you would not they should do to you." This was only a refrain. It was a rule telling us what to avoid doing. The grand old Plato went further, and in a kind of prayer, says, in the eleventh book of his Dialogues, "May I being of sound mind do to others as I would that they should do to me."

Thus in the long past this heavenly maxim gave frequent signs of its coming, and as the returning sun in the arctic zone after months of night begins to utter prophecies upon the horizon, so the golden rule began far back, and after a long night, to paint glorious prophecies upon the borders of man's moral night. All who have looked over history will, however, remember now what an immense difference there is between the first hint of a law or truth and the final enthronement of the principle in the public heart. All literature of the church from Augustine to Luther, twelve hundred years, was full of Reformation ideas. Luther did not discover anything. He was not the first to express a single doctrine or fact. He was not the second, nor the tenth. Not a generation passed between Christ and the sixteenth century wherein some one did not come forward with the ideas which Luther afterward gloried in; and yet between these and Luther there lies an infinite distance created by the absence of individual elements such as Luther possessed, and the unfitness, unreadiness of society. To find the glory therefore of a truth you must not pause with the man who may have first announced it, for he may have had no conception of its worth and may have given it little love, like the Sibyl who wrote prophecies which she did not herself understand, and which, written upon leaves, she permitted the winds to carry about never to be seen or cared for again. In order to locate the glory of discovery you must measure the heart and mind that first took hold of the idea or law in its infancy or later life. You will find the word liberty in Cæsar's history and in Cicero's ethics, but they knew nothing of the idea as compared with that conception of the word in the mind of a Wilberforce or a Polish exile.

There being such a vast difference between the utterance of a truth and the enthronement of it in men's hearts, we must cast our chief offerings of gratitude at the feet of that One who had the goodness and greatness needed to hurl this law into life. Toward the golden rule Christ sustains this relation: He translated a principle into a law of every day and of every place and of every man, and then, by a strange power, and by a life and death of wonderful import, He hurled this world of love right into the bosoms of men. What other ages may have said or dreamed fades before the passion and grand uprising of that divine soul in Nazareth. In order to make this Savior seem great as possible in the minds of the common people, the pulpit often seems to desire all inquiry to pause in the sacred text, and there find all science, all agriculture, all pleasures, all policies, all doctrines. It desires mankind to think of the world as having begun all action with the voice of John in the wilderness. But this is a suppression of the truth that makes infidels of thousands of youth who are left to battle with strange questions in later life with learned men in the street, and in the halls of science and learning. Christianity needs no *suppressio veri.* It needs no art, no subterfuge. What it needs most of all is the open light of day, and the most perfect frankness of friend and foe. The facts seem to be these: The golden rule had tried long to grow up out of the human mind and spirit, and thus for thousands of years the soul stood prophetic of a Jesus. Upon a stormy sea the soul had long hung out signals of distress, and at times had dreamed it saw a harbor of refuge. In Plato it bowed in prayer for perhaps what seemed above mortality, but the storm continued and the prayer died away. If now Christ came to answer the long-flying signal of distress, to make more universal a prayer that seemed too good for even one, if He came to answer the longing wrung out of the heart by the agony of long injustice, and if by lifting the world up He made their foreheads touch these divine letters, that is glory enough, especially for the Meek and Lowly One, who came not to seek applause, but to bring a salvation, and wear, if need be, a crown of thorns.

It is enough that at Christ the great law sprang into life, and became not a philosopher's dream, but the constitution of a new civilization. Our national idea that man has an inherent right to life, liberty, and the pursuit of happiness, can be found in all the poetry of the world, from the Zend Avesta to Cowper's Task; but the great day of the idea dawned when a great nation, covering a continent, and destined to count soon a hundred millions, wrote down this principle as the basis of a national life; dawned when thirteen States and three millions of men took their stand there and, unfurling a beautiful flag, looked up like Martin Luther and said, "So help us, God." So the coronation day of the golden rule came when that tender expression of justice crept out of the poetry of Plato, and, made sacred by Christ's life and death, quickened into being by the intenseness of a soul from Heaven, that lived not in words, but in deeds, glorified by the cross and the resurrection and a near paradise, was incorporated fully into the constitution of a kingdom larger than America, embracing nothing less than the globe, and raising for its flag God's banner of love, to wave on two shores — the here and hereafter. This was the grand unveiling of this masterpiece of spiritual art.

But we pass away from this awarding of merit to speak further of the law itself.

You all know how near and dear a thing one's own self is. The moment we step away from our own consciousness we lose our mental grasp upon the phenomenon of right or wrong. We can look upon a suffering man sick or wounded, with comparative peace, because our knowledge will not travel away from our own consciousness. We may say, "Poor man, poor child, we pity thee," but we are so cut off from his pain that an infinite gulf lies between our feelings and the sufferer's agony. But let that pain, that sickness, that dying come to self, and how quickly the heart measures all the depths of the new sorrow? Oh, what a teacher is one's own breast! It is now reported that one of the victims of the Cuban massacre offered a million dollars if the savages would spare him his life. The death of others, the common calamities of life had not filled with tremor that heart naturally brave; the grief of death at large had been, as it were, spoken in a foreign language not to be understood by him, but now the grim monster was coming up against self, it was his heart that was to be pierced with balls, not yours, nor mine, but his own, bound to earth, to friends, to country, to home and its loved ones; his was to pour out its blood and sink into the awful mystery of the grave. This was the vivid measurement of things that made the hero try to buy sunshine and home and sweet life with gold. When it comes to any adequate measurement of life's ills or joys, the only line which man can lay down upon the unknown is the consciousness within, the verdict of this inner self.

The golden rule, therefore, surpasses all formulas of justice by bringing the case before this loving, trembling, sensitive self, and begging that it be tried in the light and justice of all this light of self-love, self-joy and self-agony. Had the captives of the Virginius fallen into the hands of men who had come to that culture which can see the misfortunes of others in the light of one's own misfortunes, they would have been held as prisoners of war, or as criminals worthy at least of deliberative action; but falling into hands destitute of a divine consciousness to which to refer, their fate was the one that is meted out alike by the savage of the forest or the tiger of the jungle. Before man comes to the golden rule of arguing from a noble self outward, or after, by vice, he has obliterated it, we may well leave it to Darwin to determine whether he is man or is still in the domain of the brute. The colosseum at Rome, where eighty thousand poets, orators and citizens gathered to see innocent men fight with each other and die; gathered under the eye of such barbarism that when brothers met in the arena and did not possess the nerve to pierce each other's hearts, they were urged to the fray by red-hot rods pressed upon their naked bodies; this horrid chapter that defames the human race, came from the absence of the justice which measures pain by our own pain, and happiness by our own happiness; that justice that travels from self outward, and makes the sorrow of others ours, and their happiness our happiness. In the reign of Trajan, ten thousand men thus fought. But what is it that has dispersed that mighty throng of Roman spectators? What is it that has made that marble house, where eighty thousand people could, by scores of stairs and arches, assemble or disperse in a half-hour, a solitude, and has permitted the rains of many centuries to wash out the blood marks, or hide them with ivy and flowers? The religion that began at Nazareth, and taught man to measure another's rights and sufferings by his own; this is the philosophy that at last made the gladiators throw down their swords, and take each other's hands in presence, not of a colosseum, but of a world. The howl of wild beasts died away from the amphitheater when this rule was spoken by the Savior. Beneath the liberty of to-day that has spread from America to England, and from England to France and even

Spain, and which has made kingdoms differ little from republics; beneath the freedom of slaves; beneath the public education of children, and the emancipation of woman, flows this simple principle, "What ye would that men should do to you, do ye even so to them." Such is the full acquaintance man possesses with self — such a quick and perfect realization has he of his own aversion to pain and love of happiness, that civilization may date its rise in the hour when man brings cases of duty up to this court in his own bosom.

In order, however, to render the golden rule successful, it is necessary that one have within him the cultivated attributes of manhood, for if his self be that of a savage he can learn little within. But the truth is, the civilized world has, for the most part, a noble consciousness, capable, in occasional hours, of talking in the language of the sky. Rough though the life may be, there is within a full acquaintance with the meaning of such words as pain, grief, joy, sadness, purity, repentance. Is there a heart where this sunshine and shadow do not play like alternate day and night? All possess this form of supreme assize in their own bosom, and hither, Jesus Christ says, bring your business life, hither bring your enemies, hither your friends, hither bring the orphan child, hither the father, hither those without God and hope, and decide upon duty in the sanctuary of your own heart, where your own anguish or joy has in past days spoken to you with trumpet or angelic tongue.

I am unable to fathom the financial causes and effects that come here and there in the course of time. Like the wind they come we know not whence, and go we know not whither. But while this whole question is too large and too obscure for the pulpit, and foreign to its office, yet after a financial storm has come, and thousands, almost millions, of the poor feel its hard, cold breath; when riches do not differ much from bankruptcy, we do know that the time has come for the golden rule to assume the person of an angel and move about the streets from landlord to tenant, from bank to street, and from tenant to landlord and street to bank, from palace to hovel, until the darkness shall be made light by a reciprocity that began in Christ when the human rose to the divine. It is probable God disturbs the surface of society constantly by pestilence or fire or revolutions, that his children may not live wholly for food and furniture, but may be brought face to face with the noble principles of soul, and thus be transplanted from a market-place to the world of mind and spirit. If financial success were the chief end of man, then all these defeats in the battle of gold would be a loss of labor and life indeed; but if so be that the chief thing about man is his soul's character, then any calamity that abates material progress and throws the heart back upon itself as related to man and God must be accepted as an act of a benevolent Father of all. It is said that the dusty droughts which once in a few years dry up the grasses, grains and flowers, and make a garden land a desert, are Nature's beneficent resort, that the earth being thus ridden of all her moisture, the sunshine and air may enter the labyrinth and re-make by their new agencies those cells to which the roots of the verdure will descend in the subsequent years, and over that desert of one summer there will wave seven summers of richer harvest. In the history of morals and religion there comes a similar phenomenon in each group of years. Something called a public calamity spreads over country and home, making a desert of what was yesterday a paradise; but if we assume that the chief end of man is the attainment of a noble character, then what are these calamities but hours in which the great human world is stripped of its vanity, that its soul may lie open to the air and sunlight of a kind God coming with the music of laws for which the soul was made, and without which it is hopeless poverty. These sublime laws of life, of which the golden rule is only one, ought to lead us all to feel that grand must be the ideal destiny of man when Christ has flung down beneath him such laws of ascent, pointing to the perfection of heaven. If the ladder that sprang up before Jacob in his dream, pointing up to the stars, with angels on its steps, was any hint to him and all who read the dream that there is a world above this, then these laws of human action, so lofty, and bringing a consciousness so sweet, should seem as it were a ladder with angelic spirits upon the steps, waving their hands upward and pointing out the destiny of the soul.

RIGHTEOUSNESS.

SERMON III.

RIGHTEOUSNESS.

"Thy right hand is full of righteousness."—*Ps. 48 : 10.*

MEN of learning, such as Mill and Comte and Spencer, and men of science have said so much of late that seems to separate human virtue from relation to God, that I desire this morning to speak upon the apparent relation between religion and a correct life.

It is probable that no other important term revealing an attribute of God and man, occurs so often in the Scriptures as this word righteousness. As in science there are great terms, such as development, causation, agencies, constantly recurring, showing the central spirit of the science; so in religion at large, the word righteousness is constantly upon the page. It must follow from such a perpetual presence of this term, that religion and righteousness are closely allied. God, who is the source of religion, is seen by the inspired poet to have his right hand full of righteousness. In the classic pictures of the gods, some held in the right hand an olive branch, some a scepter, Neptune a trident, Apollo arrows, Mercury a wand, Minerva a scroll, Venus a golden apple. It is a proof of superiority in this picture from the Psalmist that his Deity seemed to reach forth a right hand full of righteousness.

Our theme this morning will be the fellowship between righteousness, or virtue, and religion.

The word right comes through all the civilized languages without much change, from an old classic radical, signifying straight or true to a rule. When the old mason found his work answering to the plumb line, he said *rectus;* or answering to his level or to his model, he said *rectus.* The significance of the term is therefore found in the material world, where something is found to conform to a perfect standard. The termination, "ous," always means full of, abounding in, from the Latin *osus*, as dolorosus, full of grief, undosus, covered with waves. Hence righteousness signifies abounding in, conformity to a moral ideal, full of correspondence to some perfect rule of action or being. Religion has a less clear significance. When we have said that it is a spiritual binding of man to God, we have said all we know about the word's primitive significance. Its actual import is that of human friendship toward God. The relation between man and man is called society; between man and country is called patriotism; between man and beauty is called taste; between man and God is called religion. Hence religion is perceived to be a sentiment, while righteousness is a mind and soul full of action, conformed to a perfect or lofty rule. The relation of religion and righteousness at once becomes evident. Religion helps the mind to a higher ideal, and helps it to a desire and power to reach in action such an ideal in thought. Just as one's love of country helps the mind to study the best path of conduct toward that country, and then urges forward to action, so religion helps the mind to become a student of righteousness, and then helps to the spiritual power that will perform deeds abounding in this fitness *to* the ideal.

In order to appreciate the topic offered to your thoughts to-day, it will be necessary for you to recall the history of unrighteous conduct, if only you could do so. But in thinking of this dark sea that has surrounded mankind, you perceive at once that there is no line long enough to sound the gulf of cruelty, of dishonor, that lies between man's origin and the present hour. History resounds with the clanking of chains and the screams of the dying. Force was the original guide of mankind. Whether Carthage or Babylon or

Jerusalem should be destroyed, and their citizens put to death, were always questions of ability to do so. No ancient sword was ever stayed while it had power to kill, or victim to be killed. The number of human beings killed by Julius Cæsar is placed at one million two hundred thousand, and the number of lives put to death by the Conquerors of Jerusalem is placed at three million men, women and children. From the earliest history to the most recent centuries, the terrific events of the world have not been seen where pestilence or flood, or earthquake or famine came, but where man marched, carrying chains for the slaves, deeper poverty for the poor, deeper pain for the suffering. Man has been a worse foe to man than have all the beasts of the forest, and all the storms or famines or plagues in nature.

The scientific minds are trying to show that the human race has been living upon this earth for a half million years, coming up slowly in all that long flight of time. But I am not sure that Mercy ought not to hope all such estimates to be false, for when we remember what man has been in the historic period we cannot help hoping that the six thousand years are all, and that there were no myriads of ages before of cruelty still less merciful, of barbarism still more barbarous. Unrighteousness is the great foe of the human race.

Issuing from private life and injuring our neighbor, or issuing from the bench and perverting justice, or issuing from the legislature and grinding a community, or issuing from a pope or inquisition and torturing the innocent; or issuing from a throne and making a nation drip in blood, unrighteousness has always been the chief sorrow and disgrace of man's career upon earth. If one will sit down with this black history open before him, how beautiful upon its background will all deeds of righteousness appear, deeds that conformed to infinite right of neighbor. Whether you recall all the tenderness there has been in the world between parents and children, between friends, between rulers and subjects, and the justice of law and of courts, each fact will reveal at once the divineness of righteousness, its whiteness, its sweetness.

In estimating the worth of right, it is a great mistake if you limit this righteousness to the obedience of statute or common laws. Such limitation gives an honest man or a law-abiding citizen, but not a righteous man, for righteous means abounding in right, in fitting, in appropriate action. When you watch by the bedside of the sick, or teach the ignorant, or comfort the sorrowful, or give to the helpless poor, you are acting righteously, because there are unwritten laws of humanity; there is an ideal law out of the statute, and above the statute, to which the deed conforms, and from which secures its title of righteousness.

So far back as Sophocles the existence of such ideal law was confessed. The beautiful character, Antigone, unveils the fact in these lines.

> No ordinance of man can ere surpass
> The settled laws of nature and of God,
> Not written these on pages of a book;
> Nor were they passed to-day or yesterday.
> We know not whence they are, but this we know,
> That they from all eternity have been,
> And shall to all eternity endure.

When the humane woman of our age reveals the spirit of this Greek sister, and flies to the hospital of Scutari or Memphis; when Grace Darling launches her boat upon the mad water, these go at the command of righteousness; for the human heart tossing in anguish in the hospital, or struggling for life in the sea, is surrounded by divine right to the helping hand; rights which may escape the coarse mind, as the brute world cannot see the rainbow nor enjoy the flowers beneath their feet; but rights which in God or the soul like God, are as vast as the constitutions of States. When the great Justinian defined justice 1500 years ago, as "a constant and urgent wish to render to every one that which is his own," did he mean only that man must respect landmarks and pay debts? Oh, no! but when a man is struggling for life in the waves, your hand ceases to be your own; it becomes partly his. All your powers for the moment belong to him. In the agony of death he is surrounded by tender rights. No other definition of justice would have been handed down by the bar and bench for 2000 years, as worthy of Justinian or of legal philosophy. Between such a justice and righteousness there is no difference. Hence we perceive that righteousness is a most perfect and most delicate perception of the rights of others, and a constant and urgent wish to bless others by regarding these manifold rights. Righteousness is a conformity to all the large or tender laws of humanity; true to them as the stars to their path. How grand a principle in human nature this righteousness may be, one may read by looking back at the sacred names of the past and by seeing that the most sacred are those that were most honorable. From Fabricius to Washington, from the blessed Savior down to the honest tinker Bunyan, or to the obscure dairyman's daughter, there is no radiance of earth so bright as that which shines from a name crowned with the halo of justice. The luster of riches, of office, of beauty, soon fades, compared with this sun of virtue set eternally in the heavens.

Having now asked your attention to righteousness, to its significance and scope and beauty, let me ask you to think of the partnership that exists between it and religion.

Whether there could be high and correct action without religion, I am unable to say. I know of no data from which to draw a conclusion. The world has never made the experiment, for religion has always rushed to the field so early in all national life, that man has never been able to know what he might have done without that element. Blair, long ago, said: "You may discover tribes of men without policy or laws or cities or arts, but not without religion." Plutarch had said the same. "That, traversing the world, you may find towns with out walls, without letters, without kings, without coin, without schools, without theaters; but a town without a temple of prayer no one ever saw." Hence it seems that the nature of man is such that it will never give science an opportunity to learn how perfect a righteousness there might be without the influence of a God. And as for individuals, it is perfectly impossible for them to empty their minds of the influence of their country and ancestors; and hence if you could find an atheist who has a delicate sense of justice, it would be impossible to determine how much or how little of this justice had come from a state or from ancestry that were more deeply religious. The experiment of human uprightness divested of religion can never hope to be tried. Now, how comes it that, as a fact, a sense of righteousness and a belief in God appear simultaneously and invariably in higher forms of society. Is it an accident? As well might we say that the sunshine and the harvest-field are only simultaneous events, a meeting by accident of prairie and June. The real truth must be that the appearance of God and human honor are related as inseparable companions, causing each other's life and growth. God's right hand is full of righteousness, and the right hand of righteousness is full of God. As a fact, all those who have been the students or servants of right have been believers in God. The benevolent men, the judicial men, the statesmen, the moralists, the philanthropists have all been quite free from the atheism that has always been a camp follower of the naturalist. It is the chemist, the geologist, the physiologist that most generally moves away from the idea of God, because the measurement and weight of a skull will no more lead to an ideal spirit than will the weight and measurement of an apple or a bunch of grapes. Hence, from the day when Lucretius, two thousand years ago, wrote his poem to show how worlds and things came, down to Huxley's last work, the tendency has been for the scientific mind to pause in the laws of development, and for the personal God to recede. But, meanwhile, all the toilers in the domain of right, from Justinian to Webster, from Plato to Grotius, from Solomon to Franklin, have been near and firm in their friendship for the Divine idea. The bench and bar of all countries and cities and towns, have always been allies of the faith in a God. They have not been sectarians in church always, because their habits of thought and hunger for evidence have been too large to permit them to be narrow in creed, or credulous as to a thousand dogmas; but as to the belief in a God of infinite righteousness, the whole judicial multitude, judge, lawyer, statesman, has been pervaded by the religious element. That there are lawyers who have only used law for gain, and have never studied deeply, nor loved deeply their profession, is evident; and so there are clergymen who preach only for a reward of money; but in measuring a profession, such men must be left out. Doing this, we affirm that the legal profession has always stood firm by the idea of an Infinite God. If you will cause to pass under view the great names in the department of law in all its forms, from Justinian to Puffendorf and Blackstone, however large you may make the enumeration, you will find God standing in the midst of the philosophy of each individual. When you wish to find righteousness elaborated from dust, generated from chemical action, you must go to the scientific school; but when you desire to see righteousness derived from the right hand of God, you need not go to the clergy, but may go to those who study justice, and cast themselves, not upon man's dust, but upon man's integrity. "True religion is the foundation of society." This is not from Huxley, but from Edmund Burke. "Religion is a necessary element in any great human character." This is not from Darwin, but from Webster. We mean no insult to the students of science, but mean that, as a fact, the study of law has always led the mind toward the Deity, and has thus revealed the causal connection between right and God. Passing away from the facts of society, let us listen to reason, pure and clear. God is the thought, the Being that stands as the ideal of right; and hence, the being attached to God by that chain which we call religion, stands near the fountain of right, and receives its flood into his bosom. God is the only ideal of right. This being so, the Christian, whose life is marked by deeds of unkindness, or injustice, or indifference to mankind, has no religion worth the name, for righteousness being in the right hand of God, a personal religion without a personal justice is impossible.

When the Bible says righteousness is in the right hand of God, it indicates that that is the chief attribute of the Creator, for the right hand is the emblem of power. Hence, if the mortal has no right life, he has no relation of any value to God; and on the contrary, if his life be full of active and beautiful justice, he is not far from the glorious Kingdom of Heaven. It is almost epitaph enough for the tomb of that lawyer who died a few days since in our city, that his life was righteous to an extreme degree. With God and with Nazareth as the supreme ideal of right, with this ideal daily approached by a life-long study and application of the principles of justice at the bar, with a daily increasing hatred of injustice, and growing appreciation of its power to injure, and of the power of goodness to bless, Mr. Fuller left a name that will always seem sheltered from hate and preserved for love by that Right Hand on High, full of righteousness. His memory is wreathed with those flowers of justice at the right hand of his God.

"No man's religion," says South, "ever survives his morals." This must be so, for as no artist could paint or carve or sing, after his ideal of color or form or sound were taken away, so no man can be called religious whose ideal of righteousness has fallen into the mire of the street. We can always measure our religion by our virtue. God is the embodiment of the idea of infinite and tender justice. Hence, as the ocean lies by our continent, the source out of which spring our rain clouds, that water the fields, and the warmth that softens our climate, so the name of God lies away from man, the perpetual source of all justice, all love, all charity — the sea out of which rolls virtue's golden cloud and vernal air.

Always, in all places, I think there is to be found the phrase on the lips of suffering: "Help me for God's sake; for God's sake give me food; spare my children for God's sake." What is the meaning of this old, old appeal that has followed human life everywhere in all its wanderings? It is only this. There is an infinite regard for rights with God. With Him the slave is as good as a king. A little child hungering, a poor father carried to the dungeon for a debt, are fully within the Infinite pity. He has laws of help and of release. And then regarding his laws, he never slumbers nor sleeps. The Divine heart redoubles the number of human rights, and redoubles the watchfulness over these laws; and hence "save me for God's sake" is a petition that begs us tear our dead hearts away from the customs of men, and rush into the righteousness at the right hand of the Infinite One; begs you to rise above the human level and look down upon me and upon my children from the tender skies of God. In my extreme hour, go away from man and look upon me from the throne of the Blessed One.

Religion creates righteousness by leading the mind daily up to this sublime ideal, by tearing the heart away from State laws or customs, and placing it by the Holy One above. Where the slave systems prevailed, masters took their stand by the statute law of the American or of the Mosaic age, or both; while those who overthrew the system, took their stand above State law, far up in the atmosphere of the Almighty, and the slave found liberty in God's right hand.

But religion has still another relation to righteousness. To the divine ideal of right it adds a varied and powerful motive. It so defines life, so limits it here, and expands it hereafter, that it forces upon us the conviction that nothing but a tender righteousness is worth living for in these years. It assures us that we shall soon go home, carrying with us no gold, no office, no fame, nothing but the lines black or white graven in the spirit. The tomb is before us. Nature has seen to it that we shall not one of us escape. Science tells us perhaps we shall pause forever there; but religion opens other gates, and makes this life a mere daybreak of the matchless world to come. But its unavoidable theory is that the spirit only shall be welcome there. All the rank and gains of this world remain behind. The soul goes with its character alone, as the bird flies to the tropics, taking with it only its companions and its song.

Not only does this obliteration of these material things drive the human race logically towards character, but the solemnity of death, and the grandeur of immortality transform righteousness into a sentiment, an inspiration, and thus make the heart burst forth into good deeds, as the eye of parting friends fills with tears. When the passenger ship is sinking in mid-ocean, the hearts about to perish overflow with kind deeds toward each other, not because the ideal of justice has come down to them from the skies only, but because the receding earth and the rapidly coming eternity, have exalted their ideal into a profound sentiment; have baptized duty in a sea of love and self-forgetfulness.

By holding God up before mankind, religion furnishes a glass in which one may always see a justice wider and tenderer than any which a godless world might give; and then by the exclusiveness of the life to come, which invites nothing from earth but its virtue, and by the beautiful solemnity of death and immortality which transforms justice into a mother's love, restless and measureless; religion, thus equipped, takes her stand by the side of righteousness, to stand hand in hand, inseparable forever. Hence it would seem that there is no virtue without religion and no religion without virtue.

The inferences from this dependence of human purity upon God, must be these:

(1) Christ, in unfolding the character of God, in tearing down all idols, and in filling the Universe with one spirit, infinite and blessed, has done a work that should bind Him upon the forehead and heart of man.

(2) If God is the ideal of justice, it becomes the Christian world to see to it that His character is so painted that the human mind can look up to Him and feel the grandeur of the ideal, not to be repelled, but charmed and conquered. The Blessed Name must be divested of the charge of having created millions of beings in order that he might damn them forever. He must be so set forth that mothers will not bow in agony over a dying child, lest, unbaptized, it might be lost eternally from their bosom. The Blessed Name must be freed from the whole terrific associations of ages of cruelty and brute force, and so set before mankind in the spotless robes of justice, that the human heart, sinful or virtuous, shall always feel the Divine presence and beauty; that there is a holy and powerful God pervading all the hours of time, and eternity.

I have avoided any Bible argument this morning, because I wanted to show you the basis of the Bible itself. There is a common impression that the Bible has created a religion for man by a positive enactment. This is partly true; but there is a deeper, broader truth; and that is, that there is a relationship of man and God that has created the Bible. The Bible has not made religion, but religion and righteousness have made the Bible. Christianity is not forced upon us. Our own nature has forced it up out of the spirit's rich depths. As the hidden music of the old fabulous statue became vocal when the sun arose each morning upon it, so when Christ came he only awakened to its divinest strains a music whose origin was far above and back of Bethlehem and the cross.

CHRISTIANITY AND DOGMA.

SERMON IV.

CHRISTIANITY AND DOGMA.

"If any man will do His will he shall know of the doctrine, whether it be of God or whether I speak of myself." —*John 7 : 17.*

CHRIST uttered these words just after He had unfolded what seemed to Him great doctrines in religion; and fearing lest the multitude might suppose He was only uttering sudden human conceptions, after the fashion of the walking philosophers, or raving sibyls, He informed them that if they would practice His teachings they would discover them to be great laws of God. I have read this declaration of Christ, not so much because it suggests how mankind may determine which doctrines are true, but also what truths are worthy of being honored with the name of a doctrine of God. The truth of an idea, and the value of an idea, are two different things, and this text is announced before you this morning because it submits to us a method of learning, not only the truth of propositions, but the relative value of propositions. If mankind can learn by experience what doctrines come from God, then the lawful inference is, that the great doctrines of Christianity are open to the test of this human experience; and further, that those propositions which are beyond the reach of man's daily life were not in Christ's mind when He discoursed to men upon the way of salvation.

This theme of remark is rendered appropriate in these days by the wonderful amount of complaint which is heard upon all sides against dogma, and by the almost equal amount of defense which dogma receives at the hands of the champions of formal theology. The fashionable cry of the worldling is, "I cannot accept so much dogma;" and the reply is rather too fashionable in some quarters, "He is a rationalist, a poor infidel." At least we have come to days when the complaint against dogma is loud and long. It is possible that much of this war of words comes from a conflicting use of terms, that the skeptical generally mean by "dogma" certain accidents of Christianity, and seldom the cardinal principles of religion; while the theological minds understand by "dogma" all the doctrines of their faith, and hence rashly use the word "infidel" regarding many who are as near as themselves to the form and soul of Jesus Christ. It will generally be found, upon conversing with these enemies of dogma, that they are thinking of the decrees of the Church more than of any of the great laws of Christianity; and instead of gazing at the Son of God and of man, are entangled amid the blue laws of New England, or the hundreds of deliverances of the councils of the Protestants and old Catholics. Often when the German free-thinking young man is declaiming against dogma he is thinking only of the Puritan Sabbath and of the hostility of the Church to his drinks and recreation.

That there is a vast amount of opposition to the whole of Christianity and religion is painfully true, but there is also a vast amount of ill-will developed by, and exhausted upon, ideas that have come from men rather than from God, or at least have been expanded by sectarian force into a significance far beyond the warrant of Infinite wisdom. When we remember that there was a time — and perhaps that time includes the present practice — when some branches of the Scotch Church had run the number of their decrees up into the thousands; and when we remember what attitudes our home denominations have taken regarding amusements, or music, or street-cars on Sunday, or dress, or psalmody, or communion, or immersion, we ought to feel that a wicked world may often speak disrespectfully of dogma without being either deficient as to common sense or hopeless as to religion. If our Protestant world does not furnish us with adequate illustration of what the world generally means by dogma, we can look across at the Roman Catholic spectacle, and see in their Immaculate Conception and Infallibility and Real Presence, specimens of the kind of doctrine which the much-deceived world has at last come so greatly to fear. Not only for the wicked world's sake, but for the Church's own sake, for its growth in greatness of mind and in happiness, it should make such distinction between the fundamental laws of religion, which may be tried by experience, and the notions which are wholly beyond such a test, as to free itself from the necessity of expelling a man who sings a human composition, as in the case of Mr. Stuart, or of withholding fellowship from those who may not have been immersed, or who may not have enjoyed the hand of a Bishop upon their forehead. While such things are constantly transpiring, we need not wonder if a wise age, looking on, says, not "We are weary of religion," but "We are weary of dogma." Unless by dogma the complaining world means the accretion which has been cast upon the shores of the Church by the turbulent sea of debate and sectarian interest, its fault-finding has no logical basis. After a man, or a handful of men, have conceived the idea of rallying around some notion, such as Immersion, or Decrees, or Ability, or Inability, that notion soon comes to represent capital, and pastorates, and schools, and seminaries, and publications, and holds then all the power of an empire *de facto.* It must be against these Church governments founded in the *coup d'etat* of individuals, that the outside multitude is aiming its chief assault, for that men of intelligence should declaim against doctrine in Christianity, is beyond belief. As none of these cultivated skeptics come to Nature and ask her to produce a floral world without any laws of rain and soil and sunshine, so they certainly do not come in their rational moments to Christianity, and require that the vast world of its morals and spirituality shall grow up without possessing any laws of cause and effect. Does the boasting rationalism become supernatural at last, and expect the realm of virtue and piety to come from nothing, and depend upon nothing, and possess no possible order of sequence? We conclude otherwise, and submit the proposition that no man can preach Christianity without being a doctrinal preacher, and no man can acquire a Christian or a religious heart, except by the obedience of doctrine. Doctrine sustains the same relation to Christian character and hope that mechanical law sustains to the cathedral of St. Paul, or that the law of sound sustains to the church chimes or the music of the many-voiced organ. The attempt to separate Christianity in any way from its own announced doctrines, is as pitiable a weakness as it would be to invite engineers to bridge a vast river by emotional action, wholly separate from any creed of mechanics.

Having reached the inference that Christianity is founded upon doctrine, that doctrines are its state laws, and that all preachers must be doctrinal preachers and all Christians doctrinal Christians, let us look now into the quality of these doctrines which all must teach and obey. When we shall have found these, we shall have escaped the thing which the wicked world fears or suspects — a group of human dogmas supporting some Church *de facto*, secured by a usurpation in some dark night, and shall have found what the wicked world ought to love — a Church *de jure*, founded by the Almighty and sanctioned by the longings of the soul and by the experience of all generations. In seeking for these doctrines we may permit Christ, the Founder of Christianity, to supersede reason and point out a path for his followers.

But the moment He has uttered our text — that "Those which men can subject to experience are the doctrines that be of God," reason rises up and unites its voice with that of simple authority. The doctrines of Christianity are those which may be tried by the human heart. This is declared often in the Divine Word. From the words of Solomon, "Fear God and keep His commandments, for this is the whole duty of man," to the Savior's words of the text, from the psalm, "O taste and see that the Lord is good," to the deeply spiritual passage where Christ compares Himself to bread to be eaten by the soul, there is one prominent idea — that the doctrines of religion are those which can be converted into spiritual being, making the spirit advance from childhood to the statue of Christ. With such a measuring line in the hand it would seem easy for any one to discover which are the great laws of Christianity, and what are only the facts or alleged facts of the religion. The difference between a fact and a law is perfectly obvious, but yet it is often necessary to remind mankind of things that are obvious. For example, singing of psalms and immersion may have been actual facts of the Bible times. It is most probable immersion was the fact of the New Testament, and yet neither of these facts can be made a Church law or a Church doctrine, because it is not possible for human experience to distinguish here, and to taste and see that the Lord is any more truly good through immersion than through sprinkling, or through a psalm of David, than through the Christian hymns of Wesley or Watts. In the great empire of experience it is the spirit in the baptism or in the song only which can so much as exist, and hence it is the worshipful spirit alone which becomes a part of religion's great law. But when the Bible says, "He that believes shall be saved," it unfolds a doctrine; for human experience, taking up this faith, is wholly transformed thereby, as a desert is transformed by rains and sun into a paradise. Faith is man's relation to Christ, just as the student's love of knowledge is his relation to all study and wisdom. Faith is the union between the cluster and the vine, between the rose and the nourishing earth. Separate the rose, and it withers — never reaches its bloom. Hence he that believeth not is damned, because, the chain that should have bound him to God being broken, his moral world sinks and goes out in the darkness, like the virgin's oilless lamp when the joy of the marriage feast was near. If God is the life of the world, then the soul that separates itself from Him by unbelief would seem to have broken the chain of perpetual being. Hence some infer the annihilation of the wicked, others their loss of happiness, rather than of existence. Be the details what they may, faith is not a doctrine like that of Immersion or of Decrees, an idea beyond appreciation; but is one which, like the law of food and drink, lies wholly within the daily life of the soul. Such also are the ideas of repentance and conversion, and of a mediatorship, and of the divineness of Christ. These cannot, except by the most thoughtless or else the most unjust, be counted as dogmas in the contemptuous sense, for they are seen at once to be phases of human experience — forms of its daily life, of its regrets, of its reforms, of its confidence, of its hopes. A world which demands of men apology when insult is offered; a public reason which asks that a political rebel shall become penitent and shall become converted as to the national flag, ought not to banish penitence and conversion from the empire of God, that great fatherland of the soul.

Appealing, therefore, to the range of human experience, we must declare faith, repentance, and conversion, to be unavoidable laws of Christianity, not having come into it by any council of Catholics or Protestants, but direct from God, who poured into the human mind its reason, and into the heart its love. Not so easily can we persuade Reason to admit, as a matter of public experience, the idea of a mediator. We waive the inquiry as to Reason's voice, because we are seeking not what the public confesses, but what Christianity itself holds, that may perchance be a matter of experience, may be "tasted" and thus be seen to be good. Under this head, of doctrine open to experience, we must include the notion of a mediator, for we find millions of hearts glad in the feeling that there is a daysman between them and God. Millions who have passed away, have gone after a joyful life in this mediator to a peaceful death in Him. The hymns of many ages, from the tombstones of the Christian catacombs, where a few sweet words were written, to the "Lamb of God, I come, I come," of our century, the experience of man as to the idea of a mediator, has rolled along like Danté's vast bird-song over the forest of Chiassi. When we sing the hymn, "Jesus, Lover of my soul," or "Rock of Ages, cleft for me," and look into the faces of those borne upward by this sentiment, we know that this idea of a mediator belongs to human experience, and hence is to be enrolled among the doctrines of any true Christianity. Let us approach now a more warmly disputed proposition, that the divineness of Christ is something essential in the Christian system. The Trinity, as formally stated, cannot be experienced. Man has not the power to taste the threeness of one, nor the oneness of three, and see that it is "good." Man cannot "do His will" here, and "know of the doctrine whether it be from God." It is not conceivable that any one will pretend to have experienced three persons as being one person, the same in substance, and at the same time equal. This doctrine, therefore, belongs to a simple religion of fact, and not to one of experience; and hence the distance between that idea and the idea of faith or penitence is the difference between a fact and a perpetual law. But while human experience cannot approach the Trinity, it can approach the divineness of Christ; for if Christ be not divine, every impulse of the Christian world falls to a lower octave, and light and love and hope alike decline. There is no doctrine into which the heart may so inweave itself and find anchorage and peace as in this divineness of the Lord. Hence, Christianity bears readily the idea of three offices, and permits the one God to appear in Father, or in Son, or in Spirit; but when the divine is excluded from Christ, and He is left a mortal only, the heart, robbed of the place where the glory of God was once seen, and where the body was once seen rising from the tomb, and where the words were spoken, "Come unto me ye that labor and are heavy laden," is emptied of a world of light and hope. The doctrine of "our Lord" in the New Church, which makes the Son of Man the place in the universe where the glorious presence of God becomes visible like the colors of the sun dissolved in the sunset; the doctrine of the mystical pantheist, that Christ overflows like a cup of golden wine too full, will always be holier in usefulness than any being coming up in the garments of only a poor mistaken hermit, of common poverty and common frailty. There is now a hymn, popular in the Methodist Church, at least, which begins with this line:

> Follow Me, the Lord is saying;.

and the still more popular hymn,

> Thee will I love, my joy, my crown,
> Thee will I love, my Lord, my God;
> Thee will I love beneath thy frown,
> Or smile beneath thy chastening rod;—

both of which were written by a mystical pantheist, who was grand in his conception of Christ as the place where the Deity held encampment for the joy and guidance of man. In presence of such experience, to make Christ only a frail human is to strike Christianity in its heart's life; and hence among the great laws of the Christian religion, selected by the measurement of our text, we must include the divineness of our Lord.

As a result of the principle here given, that the doctrines of Christianity are such as may be tried by experience, hundreds of what the world calls dogmas are excluded from any enumeration of essentials, and must stand only among the facts, or alleged facts, of Christian history, and not among religion's laws of life and salvation. God does not ask you to taste the tasteless, nor to experience that which lies beyond sight or sense; but to cast yourself into the laws of faith and conversion, and repentance, and love and hope, and of the Divine Lord, and upon these be carried by a new, recreative experience over to a new world called a new heart here — called heaven hereafter. If we base our religion upon a revelation, we must find in it not only the existence of a doctrine, but the relative value of a doctrine. We need not go to the Bible for a truth, and to man for an estimate of the value of the truth. The comparative value of a truth is to be learned from the guide that pretends to lead the human race. For example, if the doctrine of faith plays a more prominent part in the Bible than the doctrine of infant baptism, such also will be the order of their usefulness; and if the three offices of God, as Father and Redeemer and Spirit, are made more prominent than the idea that these three persons are one God, then what mankind will need most, and use most, will be the three influences, God as Father, God as Savior, God as Holy Spirit; and what he may make secondary is the enigma of the three in one, for why make prominent things which are not conspicuous in the inspired guide. By this estimate of Christianity, illustrated in this discourse, you who are afar off and unwilling to come nearer to this Savior, may at least find a method of discriminating between a Church weighed down by a hundred declarations, and that simple religion of Christ which announces but few laws, and those all measurable by your own experience. Two hundred years ago a pietist left the world this couplet:

> Lutherans, Papists, Calvinists abound,
> But tell me, where are Christians to be found?

The answer is easy, if any one will take as a guide the words of Christ, which limit the doctrines to those which the soul can taste. A thousand sects may all be Christian, if, far away from their Papacy or Calvinism, the myriad hearts are daily living amid those doctrines of experience which are few in number, but which are the modes of life — the soil and rain and sunshine of religion's flowery fields. If you, my friend, are giving your daily thought to the facts of Christianity, and are standing bewildered to-day amid the statements of science and Genesis about earth, or its swarms of life, recall the truth that your soul cannot taste any theory of man's origin — cannot experience the origin of man, whatever that origin may have been; but when you come to the law of love to man, and to the highest self-love, then you have come to a realm all responsive to your touch; a realm beyond the reach and inquiry of science, and the same yesterday, to-day and forever. Thus, turning from only events to the laws of Christianity, you will find in faith and love and hope, and in the presence of a Divine Lord, a world that will every year yield thee such a harvest of virtue and joy as nothing else can ever bring. Oh, skeptical friend! oh, Christian, too! fly each day from the debate over simple events or entities in religion, to the laws of being that may be tasted like sweet fruit, and which confess themselves at once to belong to the nature of God and man. It is in this realm of experience the millions of earth become one. From this sea of feelings the spirits of men rise to heaven from every shore; like golden mist, up from it ascended the form of Enoch and the chariot of Elijah, Magdalen and John; up from this living wave went the dark African, and the Catholic and the Protestant martyrs, and lifted by these arms of a sweet experience, our children, who have wholly escaped religion's isolated ideas, rise both in life and death toward God, the immortal trophies, not of dogmas, but of the laws of faith and love and worship.

EMOTION AND EVIDENCE.

SERMON V.

EMOTION AND EVIDENCE.

"I love them that love me."—*Prov. 8 : 16.*

IT must be only the affectionate seekers of truth that may expect to find the hidden prize. The Wisdom, personified by the poetic Solomon, and represented as sitting at the beautiful gates of the city, an angel of light, cried out to the passing throngs, "I will give my stores of knowledge to those who will give me their friendship." From this scene pictured by the oriental past, from this exchange of truth for love taking place between an angelic form and the unlettered multitude, I would this morning draw the lesson that the mind must reach religion's creed by help of the heart. It is not intimated thus that reason is to be set aside and that we are all to evolve information out of our feelings, and become independent henceforth of all major and minor premises, and of that whole circuitous path to knowledge; but with the value of the rational faculty exalted to its highest honor, I would ask you to believe that the affections of the heart must constantly aid the rational faculty, if it is expected to accomplish much in the realm of moral truth. Wisdom will love those who love her. That is, there must be something in the soul that will welcome what words she may speak. There must be an attuning of the two instruments, the objective truth and the subjective man, such that the music of the former may not be rejected as a discord, or lost because inaudible. It has been discovered by scientific men that the human ear is capable of hearing only those tones which are produced by some definite number of vibrations to the minute, and hence there may be a music in the woods and in the air very near, but in tones beyond the octaves possible with man, and hence that higher fact of music may not love man or reveal itself, simply because man does not love it. Leaving the region of fancy, let us return to the region of fact, and there we do without doubt perceive that Wisdom has always distributed her truths, not to those who hate her, but to those who love. She fills with her blessings those hands which are willingly and even beggingly raised. Inasmuch now as the domain of religion is the last place in which men will confess this proposition to be true, let us come to this department only after having marked elsewhere the habits of love and doctrine, or the heart and the creed.

You have all just seen a great wisdom in a certain province of study, and a great love in the same province come to a grave, and disappear. Nature told her secrets of birds, trees, fishes, sponges, and sea-weeds, to this illustrious inquirer. Along the Amazon river and amid all the chains of mountains, and on all the sea shores, the angel of wisdom, which Solomon says was with God when He gave the sea its decree, stooped to this mortal whom the world mourns, and whispered story after story of the earth's forms and changes and life. Between this subjective mortal and the objective wisdom, friendship was the perpetual days-man bringing together the world of nature and the world of soul. This naturalist only illustrates the nature of man and asks us to confess that all the children of earth who have found at last any vast information, all the old artists and poets and statesmen and philosophers from the most remote Zeno to the most near Guizot or Mill, have found their stores of truth by following the lead of a positive love for the domain of their toil. The many-colored wisdom they found loved them because they loved it. All the success of Angelo and Watt and Morse and Fulton came not in antagonism to their hearts, but under its welcome and smile.

Now, with such phenomena before us we cannot but conclude that those special ideas called "religion" will become truths or doctrines, only by help of the heart's friendship at least. Unless men can reach some wish in their favor, some partiality for them, it is hardly to be supposed that mere logic will ever force them upon individual or public practices. The power of the mind to reject conclusions not welcome to the feelings is enormous. Hence the couplet—

"Convince a man against his will,
He's of the same opinion still."

because the feelings create and color our world for us, and where they do not come to the task, our world goes back to chaos again. The fact that feelings often carry men away from truth, or beyond truth, and thus have originated the expression that "The wish is father of the thought," only shows the almost divine power of the feelings, and that if they can make even a dream seem real, how real must a truth become by the help of their enchantment? If there be some attribute of soul which can make a shadow seem a substance, that is what we all need to guard a substance from becoming a shadow. In an age which is boasting of great logical power, and which is laughing at all those emotional, thoughtless mortals who have a worship, and a faith, and a hope of immortal life, let the experiment be tried of a pure rationalism brought to bear upon a fine art instead of upon a religion, and let the result be marked. Go to the musician and tell him to put aside all emotion, demand that he join some "philosophical society," and there, by a purely mental process, determine whether what he hears is really music or only a less gross discord; require him to justify his conception of pleasing sound, detain him over the argument whether all sound is not music, or all music is not simply noise, and all the while tell him that nothing is so unmanly as any feeling upon the subject, that to have feelings is to part with philosophy; and at the end of a brief schooling of this kind you may have added to the quantity of rationalism, but you have robbed one home, at least, of its music. This illustration is not wholly fanciful, for the great Stuart Mill confessed that in his boyhood's love of music there came up constantly the fear that an end would soon be found to the possible variations of the eight notes, and then no more new music would ever be possible. Thus the shadow of an extreme rationalism began to fall upon a world of beauty, checking the impulse of the heart.

You may perceive in the world a practice commended, which, in religion, is by the same world often condemned. Thus we are told that the boy Henry

Clay so loved the pleasure and the fame of oratory that he practiced the speaker's art out in the fields, and worked among the rows of corn to the music of oratorical tones and long sentences; and this prepossession of the heart is greatly praised as being the power which carried him from the farm to the senate. Without this prepossession, it is confessed, the country would have no such name in its catalogue of loved ones as that of Henry Clay. But if that early bias of heart was valuable, it must have been so for definite reasons, and permanent reasons, in the form of permanent laws. Those laws must have been these: 1. That prepossession was the stimulus of industry. It made all toil along the given path sweet, and a pleasure more than toil. 2. It also kept the morrow roseate, so that the future of his country, and the possible future of himself, lay before him in such sunlight as to drive away from around his feet the shadow of poverty, and to feed his heart upon the manna of a far off success. The enthusiasm of this youth did not contradict logic, did not so load the young man down with follies and superstitions that it was necessary for a rigid philosophy to go to him in after-life and strip him of his sentimental frippery and lead him back to a life without dogma and without prejudice. The truth was exactly the opposite.

Through the soil of that enthusiasm the actual ideas of oratory had all sprung up. They became visible in the rich atmosphere of love. Loving those that love her the doctrines of oratory had fully revealed themselves to him who had first given her his heart. Thus the wish is often father of the thought, not only of a false thought, but most commonly of the true one. In order for a truth to rise up in its real beauty and show us its dimensions, and repeat to us all its evidence, it is absolutely essential that it stand forth in the world of our sympathy. The indifference of what is called reason will not answer. Truth will not hang her pictures in such a cold, feeble light. The atmosphere of good will, like that which in Angelo revealed the truths of his art, or in Clay the truths of his oratory, must envelop religion also and help her cardinal ideas from the formless void up into the world of life and light.

It is possible that the poverty of evidence, confessed in this world to exist as to vast moral propositions, comes from the fact that earth was made not for a wicked but for a virtuous race. Where the heart would always have been helping state and restate, and to treasure up the evidence of God and a future life, the whole moral outlook would have been clear as the existence of the sun in the sky. It is possible that sin, in its form of hostility or indifference, has in all its long history done nothing but destroy evidence by destroying the sentiments that made it visible; has taken away a world by taking away the atmosphere which rendered it a part of man's universe, within the reach of his eye or ear. Paul speaks of things which are "spiritually discerned," and hence there must be many things in religion which fade from the sight of reason because they have fallen from the spirit's tenderness — the sight of its love. In the public journals recently there was an account of the suicide of a boy of eleven years. He had been so cruelly beaten by his father in all these eleven years — for infancy had been no protection — that the gloom of death became less terrible than the anguish of torments here. The particulars are too horrible to be given. Were you empowered to transform that monster into a man, you would not dare attempt it by logic alone. To read the statutes of the whole world and the ethics of all casuists, from Confucius to William Penn, would be powerless compared with the privilege, if you could secure it, of leading that father back to a childhood of his own, and there in some kind home lay afresh the foundations to his soul. What he needs is a new soul, all out and out, in which the joyful sports of children would echo like music, and where a tear from one of them, caused by himself, would not burn their cheek so much as his own heart. Out of this new spiritual state the laws of parent and child would rise right up as visible as great verdure-covered mountains. In this atmosphere of love the laws of man to man would not be enlarged by a false mirage; they would be seen in vast outlines, because they are not atoms, but have all the magnificence of worlds. In our penitentiary, a few weeks since, there took place an event which has sickened the community into silence. There are now and then deeds done which discourage tongue and pen, and make the pulpit and press silent, not from indifference, but from sorrow and hopelessness. Now, if you were compelled to begin the education and Christianizing of the person or persons most deeply guilty of that wretched act, would you not ask of God the power to lead those task-masters, not among the world's argument, but among its scenes of love? Lead them to where Christ is proclaiming men to be brothers; to where the hungry are being fed, and the sinful forgiven; to where Wilberforce is freeing slaves, or the American world opening up its liberty and its grand asylum, and then out of this deep study and love of man ask them to see the right of the poor convict to his life, and future hopes of home and liberty. Out of such a tender prepossession of soul, the truth of duty in all its details would flame forth in illumined letters, full of justice, because full of humanity. That any man, be he a despot in a prison, or in a kingdom, should be able to perceive intellectually the rights of his subjects without himself possessing a humane heart, is as impossible as that an artist should rise to fame by a judgment alone, his heart being perfectly empty of any love of the beautiful.

From these illustrations, taken from the life of mankind at large, I must conclude that belief, the realization of truth in the moral world, is dependent upon the friendship of the heart. The exact sciences proclaim their ideas to all, and ask no favor of any kind. Be you well or ill, happy or sad, young or old, when the exact science declares that the world is round, and that water is heavier than the air, you have no choice but to accept of the words. Science asks no friendship. But not so in morals. Her truth will love only those who love her. Announcing a God, she expects your heart so to welcome the Infinite Father that out of your affection will grow up a sacred imagination which will help you feel the presence and goodness of this blessed One. This must be the reason why there seems present in all nations the traces of a religious instinct. The love of the beautiful is not more universal than the instinct of religion, and therefore we may conclude that as the love of the beautiful is in all places urging mankind forward toward the truths of that world, and everywhere gathers up the evidence and confirms it, so in the world of religion man must set forth with a friendship upon religion's side, and permit it to help him amass the evidence and reach the verdict of God and immortality. The proud intellect may despise this statement of the case, and may say that the true mind will scorn a creed that rests in any degree upon any emotion, but it is not my effort to discover an ideal method of religious conviction, but to inquire what is the existing method of earth. Could we who are here to-day in the dim twilight of faith, and who expect to go to the tomb in the same shadow, be permitted to reshape the evidences of Christianity, doubtless we should make it demonstrative, and have men learn that there is a heaven just as they learn the sum of ten tens, or the height of a hill, or the breadth of a valley. But in the absence of such power, which might at best prove a calamity, all that remains is for us to mark the actual quality of our moral realm, and doing this we cannot but perceive that its evidence, its truth, its general creed, are inseparably joined to a friendship pointing to the God which the evidence seeks. There is many a thinking man now in the late years of his life who, could he return to youthful days again, and carry with him the wisdom gained by a long pilgrimage of doubt and sorrow, would not again attempt to learn of the existence of God and a future life from "Butler's Analogy" and "Paley's Design" alone, but abandoning those pages and going into the deep-shadowed wood where the voice of cold argument might be turned into music by the diviner sentiment of the soul; or following the footsteps of men and of little children to their sanctuary, would find in their voices and upturned faces a feeling within that shapes and adorns and redoubles the evidences of religion. If God made man upright, then out of that original piety there would have rolled up each day, truth for the day, clear and welcome, clear because welcome. But if man subsequently fell into a sinful state, then with this spiritual separation the evidence would each century become less in quantity and weaker in power, and we should after a time witness a world in which the heart of a sinner would be bound to only the evidence of a saint. Depravity would be seeking conviction from proof that was arranged for a saint. Whether our world is not just such a one I leave to your personal conjecture. Be such its history or not, the lesson seems plain that no simple criticism, no simple logical force, will meet the nature of religion or the nature of man, or the wants of the soul. Somewhere in the heart's depths, and at some time to you and me, there must spring up such a willingness that religion be true, and such a loving hope and trust as will make a just balance in which the great moral world can be weighed. To our ill-will it will give no response. To our absolutely unprejudiced soul it will say just what music would say to the indifferent, or what June would say to the insensate Indian; but to the heart seeking wisdom it will come; to the one knocking, the door of this paradise will open wide. We say all these things, while remembering well that thousands have looked upon their feelings as the voice of God, and have defied all logic, and have professed to speak and act wholly by inspiration. There is a sect now in this country whose members do nothing except by an impulse of the Holy Ghost. They despise reason, and prove the existence of God, and even the divinity of Christ, by their consciousness; but this is an abnormal, insane condition of feeling, and counts nothing against the principle of our discourse, that the profoundest reason can toil justly in morals only along the path of good-will. Reason must always toil, and be led forth each day to new conquests. In a world where truth and error are mingled like the elements in a chaos, reason is a spirit brooding upon the face of the waters. But this reason must, in its work, be the most just. It must use its evidence in the atmosphere where it was placed by nature. It should be the first instinct of reason to be reasonable, and hence if moral evidence seems to ask for the assistance of human sentiment, and cannot endure ill-will and indifference, let reason then toil upward from a base of love and kind wishes and hope.

It must be the fact that moral proof asks for a spiritual prepossession that will explain why so many coming to old age or to their death chambers feel a perfectly new conviction regarding that future world so long in shadow. It is not fear that then makes eternity, with its joy or sorrow, seem real, for rarely to adult, educated minds, does coming death bring fear. It is the empire of the heart that sends forth these closing convictions about the hereafter. The pride, the glory of logic, the pressure of skepticism, the vanity of self, are all fading away under the sway of silver hair, or of disease which plucks from man all his vanity; and in the new atmosphere of love to God and man, the evidences of religion stand forth, not in an exaggerated form, but life-size, in the first sunlight they ever knew. In those last moments or last years of life, the heart begins to look onward, and to hope that the existence about to be surrendered here will be sweetly resumed beyond, and that the dear ones which all mature lives have gathered about them in a love true, and tried by long experience, will rejoin it not long hence; and out of this solemn and closing heartbeat issues not a dream of one who is delirious, but the just vision of an intellect which has at last escaped its own life-long shadows.

Now, the practical lesson from these thoughts is this: The evidences of Christianity must be weighed by a mind not averse to virtue, not averse to the being and presence of a just God; by a mind not wholly wedded to exact science, but full of tender sympathy with man, and pity for him if his career of study and love is to terminate at the grave; by a mind capable of looking away from the market-place and from the pleasure of sense, and of beholding the vast human family flashing their angelic wings afar off beyond these humble times and scenes. The evidences of Christianity must be weighed by a soul capable of sadness and of hope. Not simply must the books of theologians be read for, and the books of skeptics against, the doctrines of faith, but the genius of earth, its little children, its joys, its laughter, its cradle, its marriage altar, its deep love crushed often in its budding, its final white hair, its mighty sorrow embracing all at last from its Christ to its humblest child, in its black mantle, must be confessed in its inmost heart; then, when to such a spirit the common arguments of religion are only whispered, the sanctuary of God would seem to be founded in eternity, and men here and angels elsewhere will throng its blessed gates. While the singer of Israel stood out in the sinful street and saw the prosperity of the wicked, his feet had well nigh slipped, but when he went into the sanctuary of God it seems that a new vision came from amid the incense and the song. Not in hours of argument, my friends, but in hours of pensiveness or solitude, the best estimates, the most just, will be made by you all who have reached the noon of life.

"In some hours of solemn jubilee,
The massive gates of Paradise are thrown
Wide open, and forth come, in fragments wild,
Sweet echoes of unearthly melodies,
As odors snatched from beds of amaranth."

GOOD WORKS.

SERMON VI.

GOOD WORKS.

"Ye see, then, that by works a man is justified, and not by faith only."—*James 1:24.*

WHOEVER should undertake to find any one doctrine in which all the essentials of salvation should be contained, would have before him a task difficult indeed. The wants of the soul are many and varied. The variety and richness which prevail in nature, with its seasons, with its myriad species of plants and animals, with its waters that reveal different colors, and with its stars which shine in different lights, are an emblem of what may be expected in the spirit world; and hence in any plan of salvation that may spring up in the spiritual confines, there should be expected some such variety of action and of doctrine as would harmonize with a varied soul and a varied world. There was once a sect—and they have not all gone from earth yet—who were called Solifidians, because they expected salvation because they believed Christ would bestow, or had bestowed, upon them that great boon. This sect had condensed the whole Bible into a single sentence, and all conduct into a mental operation called belief, and hence their chief virtue must have been that of placid expectation. In hours of gratitude over the office of a Mediator, there often seems nothing in the world but Him and His cross. Comparatively, all else fades; but the reverie of the Christian is soon broken by the words, "Why stand ye here idle?" "Blessed are the pure in heart," and "Ye see that by works a man is justified, and not by faith only;" and in a moment he finds himself in the midst of a varied world, rich and beautiful as the tropics—a world in which faith in Christ is of vast moment, but does not lay waste the whole continent. The question how the mediatorial office of Christ may do all, if man must also do good works, is just such a question as is sprung upon us by the human will. How can God accomplish His will, and at the same time permit man to possess an independent, self-determining volition? I know of no method by which we can make works necessary or essential in a kingdom of perfect redemption or perfect forgiveness; but this difficulty we pass by, and, as in the case of the will, would cast ourselves upon the evident facts of Christianity and of common life; and the facts are that the Bible, from first to last, insists upon personal righteousness. Common life, or society, teaches us also that a salvation that did not insist upon virtue would be the destruction of society in all its temporal interests. If heaven could be sustained and peopled by faith without good works, earth at least could not; it would be compelled to resort to moral lives.

The doctrine of salvation by faith must therefore be so stated and held as to leave society its friend, trusting faith rather than fearing it, and must be so stated and held as to leave the other doctrines of Christianity some reason of existence. In their joy over the newly-discovered idea of salvation by the mediation of Christ, some of the divines around Luther, with Luther himself, declared that no amount of sin would imperil the soul that should possess this marvelous faith. Thus at one stroke the doctrines of regeneration, and repentance, and sanctification, and love to man are cut down as cumberers of the ground. The Bible is reduced to one sentence; its grateful music is silenced into one note, to be sounded evermore upon a single string. This cannot be wondered at, however, for the tendency of zealous minds is always to narrow the universe, and make it all flow in the channel of their almost accidental thought or taste. There are always those with whom some one doctrine has eclipsed all other truths of the Bible. The

Second Adventists possess souls full of little except the immediate coming of the Lord. Hundreds of times have they stood in white robes awaiting for His coming in the clouds in great glory. Thus all through the history of religion the limitations of the individual, the atomic quality of the soul, has always revealed itself in its selecting an atom only of God's vast truth. In religion we all verify the legend of Achilles, that, when an infant, having been placed in a room full of objects, he picked out a sword. Thus, his soul being only an atom, it was able to appreciate only an atom of the varied world. He passed by, as though they did not exist, the implements of art or industry, the emblems of music, poetry, eloquence, perhaps the ivory images of the gods, and drew forth the emblem of death and injustice. In that far-off age one of the wise men declared philosophy to be a study of death, thus telling us, not the whole truth, but that the clouds and solemnity of the grave had so impressed this one mind that to him there was nothing worthy of profound logic except the last hour of human life. Thus we all go down to the great truths of God as a child would go to a river bank, as if to empty it with its silver cup; but after all our efforts there flows onward the mighty stream unconscious of the vain mortals upon the bank. Each individual is so much less than religion, so infinitely beneath his own Christianity, that we are bound to feel that after all his wanderings in its confines there will still be almost whole continents upon which his footstep has not been, whose flora has never greeted his eye, whose bird-song has never delighted his ear. It is in such a confession of the narrowness of individuals we can best find explanation of such an exaltation of "belief" over personal virtue as has been and is yet to be seen in many places, in many minds and hearts, and in many systems also, in the great Christian Church. Many systems of doctrine are the work of individuals — places where some finite one has sat down to measure the infinite, and has supposed the universe to be all estimated and expressed when he had only been studying his own mind and heart in the mirror of his innocent fancy. Then have come the councils to adopt this measurement, and then have followed hundreds of years in which all measuring rested, and in which all went daily and repeated the words of the individual whom they had adopted as monarch while living, and as saint when dead. Whether there will ever be a creed that will do justice to the Bible, one cannot venture to predict. The world is capable of making great progress, and it loves always the forward movement; hence no one can determine what may be the ultimate result of this capability and this longing, but up to our brilliant century all the estimates of Bible doctrine have come far short of conveying to mankind the lessons taught in the Holy Scriptures. The Arminian creeds fall short of expressing the divine side of the universe, while the Calvinistic creeds come short upon the human side; the Episcopacy has perhaps too much of the external, the Puritan too little; the old Baptist and Covenanter contained too much of perdition, the liberals too much of paradise; so that upon all sides the scene is as though we had all rushed forth to see the whole universe with our one sense of sight, or to take up an ocean in the hollow of our hand. It may be that, as the Bible contains the many sides of an infinite thought, the world will always be happy to drink of the stream, but will never be able to count its drops, or see all the smiling of its waves; and that it will be necessary for us, and for all who come after us, to hold our creeds in our hands indeed, and then to say of religion, as Newton said of the universe: "I have only gathered a few shells upon the beach." The religion of man will always be larger than any measuring soul.

This long discussion may now prepare us to hear the words of St. James which so conflict with the Solifidian words of our creeds, and of the sacred Book, elsewhere in its pages. The conflict is, however, only among mortals; it is not in the book, if we confess the many-sidedness of the world of morals, but when men so define faith, or so rigidly, as to eclipse human virtue, they create a fatal discord. When men come to a verse about faith as the Jew came to his bond, determined to have the pound of flesh, Paul and James both may as well abandon the idea of teaching truths to the children of men. Faith indeed will save a soul, but faith then is not rigidly a belief; it is more, it is a friendship, for the word belief is often wholly omitted, and for whole pages the love for Christ reigns in its stead. In St. John, the word "love" quite excludes the word "faith." Faith, therefore, being a devotion to a leader, a mere belief is nothing. A man is justified by his active affections, and not by his acquiescence in some principle. Thus faith, in the biblical sense, is not a simple belief, but a mystical union with Christ, such that the works of the Master are the joy of the disciple. Works, that is, results — a new life — are the destiny of faith, the reason of its wonderful play of light upon the religious horizon. As man by his sin lost the image of God, so by faith, that is, by devotion to Christ, he is by cross, and by forgiveness, and by conversion, rewards of his love, carried back to the lost holiness. Faith is not a simple compliment to the Deity, for it is not God who needs human praise so much as it is man who needs virtue, and hence faith must be such a oneness with Christ as shall cast the spirit more and more each day toward that uprightness called "works," which man has lost, but which only God loves. Hence James truly says, a man is not justified by what he may believe, but by such a newness of inner life as may cast the soul into harmony with righteousness. Faith, as a belief and a friendship, is good, so far as it bears the soul to this moral perfection. This perfection is the city to which faith is an open way, and the only highway and gate; therefore, by the final works or condition a man is justified.

You all, in senses more or less strict, look upon the Bible as being the divine history and law of religion. It is the way of salvation. However Christian men may differ about the Bible when it speaks in the name of science, and tells how the earth was made, and when; yet when it comes to morals, there is no denying that its pages are the record of God's will as to the life and salvation of His children. Now, in that book throughout, the works of men play so profound a part that the verse of St. James seems only the reverberation of all the voices between the Genesis and the Apocalypse. The great word of the Old Testament was "righteousness." The "fear of the Lord" was the beginning of wisdom. "Fear God and keep His commandments, for this is the whole duty of man." Nowhere in all that large volume of religious law and history is there any salvation alluded to apart from uprightness. That isolated "belief," which in some recent generations became a substitute for honesty and all morals, plays no part in the volume where Enoch "walked with God," and where it was the glory of David to be a man after God's own heart, and where the sublimity of Job's character lay in the fame he had won of being an upright man that "feared God and eschewed evil." In the glory cloud of that wonderful book the voice of God itself spoke forth and said, "He was perfect and upright." "There was none like him in the earth." He was "eyes to the blind and feet to the lame, a father to the poor." His philosophy was one of works. "Evil doers shall be cut off, but those that wait upon the Lord shall inherit the earth. Verily there is a reward for the righteous." Thus all through the Old Testament there were voices of God enough to justify the words of James and clothe them with an equal inspiration. In studying this life of Job, one of the Princeton divines seems to become enamored of "good works" as opposed to belief alone, and says Job "is evidently portrayed as a model man." * * * "No account is made of ancestry, or of connection with the covenant people of God. There is no hint of his relationship to Abraham. He was plainly not one of his descendants." * * * "Evidently it is not outward associations or connections, though of the most sacred kind, that constitute the evidence and pledge of God's favor, but personal character and life. In every nation, and in every communion, he that feareth God and worketh righteousness is accepted of Him." This Princeton divine does not pause here. As though fearing he might still be giving only a doubtful sound, he proceeds to say, "The important question is not, Are you a Jew or a Gentile? Are you a member of this or that branch of God's visible church? Nor even, Are you a member of any outward body of professing Christians whatever? but, Have you personally that character which is acceptable to God, and are you leading a life that is pleasing in his sight?" These words are exceedingly valuable, not only because true, but because, coming from a great orthodox origin, they show that the heart of the most extreme champions of "faith" can no longer separate salvation from a life of honor as to God and man. Religion is confessed to be character. But does not this Princeton teacher base the salvation of Job upon his sole relation to the coming Redeemer, apart from all personal character? I have shown that in his judgment the important question is, "Have you that personal character which is acceptable to God?" Hence the "works" of St. James are a part inseparable of the great salvation, What the divine from whom we quote does say about the "Redeemer" of Job is equally liberal and equally wonderfül. He says, "God was his Redeemer; Christ, who was in the beginning with God, and was God, is ours. When Job appeals to his Redeemer, he does so without even remotely apprehending that He (the Redeemer) is the second person of the Godhead; for, of the distinction of persons in the Divine Being, and of the doctrine of the Trinity, as unfolded in the New Testament, he knew nothing." The inference from these words is certainly this: That the most devoted students of the Old and New Testaments do, in our day at least, perceive the overshadowing question to be as Dr. Green says: "Have you that personal character which is acceptable to God?" It may be impossible for all persons to see the Redeemer just alike in His relation to each soul, but in the midst of this conflict between human works and the works of the Redeemer, the heart must cling to its personal holiness as something about which there can be no doubt. In the Bible there may be some obscurity, hiding from some minds the nature of the atonement, or mediation, or substitution of one for another, but in all the Bible there is no doubt left anywhere to hang over the doctrine that "the pure in heart only shall be blessed." Passing away from the old time and the land of Job and coming to the absolute presence of Christ, we find Him not informing Nicodemus that he must cherish a state of belief, but that "*he must be born again.*" Paul is also eloquent over the "new man," the new spirit within. Hence, while the Redeemer, both of the old patriarch and of the latest Christian, may often be carrying forward His part of the great human salvation behind clouds, heavy or light—clouds which Job could not penetrate—and which hence mankind at large need not, the human side of salvation, namely, a new life and new works, lies always in a clear light; clear whether viewed from the Bible or from the crying need of society. Society, at large and in the minute, from empire to fireside, demands a religion of good works. It would permit the man of Uz to sink his Christ in the idea of God, without separating the unity into its Trinity, but it dare not permit him to turn aside from being "eyes to the blind and feet to the lame." Society could not demand that he embody exactly so much in his hymn to his Redeemer, but it was compelled to beg him to omit nothing from his principle, "to fear God and eschew evil." This was the human side of salvation, and any shortcomings there would deeply injure all the sacred interests of State and home and heart.

We are informed that God so loved the world that He sent His Son, that whosoever believed in Him should not perish, but have eternal life. This love, therefore, will not permit the world to suffer in personal goodness by relying upon external righteousness. There is nothing society so much needs to-day as, not divine righteousness, but human righteousness. For want of this our nation mourns, our cities mourn, our churches are disgraced, our very homes are often made desolate. Our land has everything except righteousness. Did any continent of either old history or of fable, did even the Atlantis of Plato, or did the fabled northland of Hesiod, where the people lived in sweet, open sunshine for a thousand years, ever reveal such glory of learning, or invention, or art, or liberty as our land proclaims in words that have escaped fable and have become clothed with reality? The people of the blessed nation described by Hesiod, lived, indeed, a thousand years each, but not amid thought and education, but only in sunshine; not in a liberty of mind and soul, but only amid sweet spontaneous fruits; not near a temple of the Most High, but only in a land where the winds were sweet, and never rose in storm. Compared with such an empire of animal sense and peace, our nation with only its three-score years for each citizen, and with its tombs and sorrows for all at last, is as the grandeur of God compared with the smile of an infant in its first vague dream. Such a republic as we dwell in this day could not have entered into classic imagination, for the fancy cannot flow beyond the possibilities of its age, and hence to antiquity a land of such liberty, of such arts, of such inventions, of such a one God, and of such a worship, was wholly beyond the best human dream. But now, what is it that comes to mar this scene? What is it that makes the humble citizen and the statesman look upon both the present and the future with a sadness that almost at times makes them glad that there is a grave before them which shall soon be to them an end of disappointed hope? There is one outlook that casts a shadow upon this great picture of human development; it is the outlook of unrighteousness. Could this land rise to a religion of "good works," the ancient dreamers might possess in peace their elysian world of perpetual sunshine, and fruits, and of thousand-year life, for this nation, crowned with the additional charm of public and private honor, would surpass all the poetry of yesterday. Each morning paper, as the facts now are, is a history of mingled glory and shame, charity and avarice, kindness and cruelty, prayer and vice. If, therefore, God so loved the world as to send His Son, He must have sent Him, not to develop man's credulity so much as man's uprightness, not to win from us the words only "I believe," but also the words, "Lord, I will follow Thee whithersoever Thou goest." The great need of the world being an honorable life, the God who "so loved it" must find in human virtue the chief arena of His love and power and grace.

In interpreting the Scriptures all our wise men assure us that the Old Testament was the shadow of the New. This we believe. But this fact commits us to the doctrine that if the Old Testament unfolded a human righteousness, that old honor must have been only a shadow of the piety and integrity to spring up in the Christian dispensation. If the New Testament is to be a place where "belief" is a substitute for a moral life, then the uprightness of Job was not a shadow of our better era; but the spectacle is reversed, and we are the waning evening of a day whose purer sunlight fell thousands of years ago in the land of Uz. But we believe in no such retrograde of doctrine. We believe the righteousness of the Old Testament only a shadow of the great unfolding of the human heart, destined to issue out of the Sermon of the Mount. If the old law said "Thou shalt not kill," it sounded only the first note in the music of a love which would do to others what it would that others should do unto it. Indeed the Gospel is a perfect overflow of justice, of honor, of kindness, of active love. Its prayer is that men may be perfect, as the Father in heaven is perfect, and the hymn that has risen up out of its divine morality is, "Nearer, my God, to Thee." But this spiritual condition will not become universal or even common, if the word "belief" is so magnified that the Church cannot see the human "righteousness" in its supreme beauty. Pulpit and pew must confess the great breadth of religion, and not fix upon some one word and say "I have found it," "I have found it," when they have only face downward drawn so near their own earth that all the other stars are eclipsed. That grand text which helped revolutionize the Christian world in the sixteenth century, "The just shall live by faith," having by its final word set us free from Romish error and despair, ought now by its initial word to help set us free from public and private neglect of a virtuous character. Saved from superstition, we at last need a salvation from vice. Religion is so broad it demands the whole verse. Such a pyramid as Christianity cannot be founded on a simple word. Who is it that lives by faith? The just! Oh, yes! The wicked, the dishonest, the cruel cannot, it seems, live by a simple belief! It is the just who thus live. It would seem, therefore, that faith is some fountain out of which the human family is to draw a more perfect character each day, and their honor, and piety, and charity are not to draw life from man, but from faith in the living God. It is works through faith that save. Now, the lessons from the text are these:

(1) Never believe any one who comes to you with Christianity condensed into any one word, be that word ever so dear and so valuable. Christianity is not in a single term.

(2) Always distrust any one who rigidly follows the letter of God's word, for thus you will be plunged into a world of discord, and the Bible will lie at your feet a harp, broken, utterly without music for the sad or happy hours of life.

(3) Take the Bible in its infinite scope, and look upon it as a universe which you may love, but cannot weigh and measure. When your will seems powerless over life and death, fly to the Divine Will, which has no weakness, and which will do all things well. When your best works fail, and you feel their worthlessness, fly to Him whose cross stands between you and God's wrath. Believe in Christ, and find peace. But when you perceive your days to be without virtue, and without charity, and without religion, read the words of

James — that a man is justified by his works and not by faith only; and let this sentence be as the thunder of God's justice all through thy sinful heart. Oh, that this many-voiced religion might sound its true music all through our country, and give us men of love, men of faith, men of hope, and men of virtue!

THE GREAT DEBATE.

SERMON VII.

THE GREAT DEBATE.

"Clouds and darkness are round about him; righteousness and judgment are the habitation of his throne."—*Psalms 97:2.*

THE death recently of the great anti-Christian critic, David Frederich Strauss, whose warfare against the Christian Church has been the longest and most radical ever waged against our religion, makes it becoming the day near the death of such a veteran enemy that something should be said upon some theme suggested at least by this great German name. Let us postpone for some future Sunday an inquiry into the nature and results of that rationalism to which this scholar gave up almost wholly his long life, and let us be content to-day with thoughts of that great religious debate of which Strauss was only a mere fragment as to form and power and duration. His loud voice only reminds us of the fact that the whole earth has always echoed with shouts for and against religion, and the dust cloud of war which, for a half-century, followed the footsteps of this German, only remind us of the general dust cloud that has followed somebody's footsteps in religion all the way from Socrates and Celsus to Spinoza and Strauss and Emerson. If there be some page in history where the religious debate stood adjourned for a season, we do not yet know of that page, but would much love to find it and make of it a special study, and derive from it an elevated form of happiness. Looking out upon the turmoil of to-day, in which a few individuals are struggling with the old and new Episcopacy, and old and new Baptists, and old and new Presbyterians, and are tossing to and fro the words "orthodox" and "heterodox," many Christians wonder what is to become of the Church, and the daily press often exults as though in a few years no public institution would remain of value to the people except the morning newspaper. But notwithstanding the turmoil of to-day, we must yet conclude that the present is peaceful compared with the past, and that the Christian Church, in essentials the same as to-day, will long bear the press daily company, and will surpass it in filling the public heart with virtue and hope.

That the boasted enlightenment of our century ought to express itself in a wider, more loving, more genteel, more Christ-like Church than we now possess, is a question that will not admit of debate, but dismissing the ideal from our mind, and remembering the past times when our ancestors burned Servetus, and cursed Galileo, and hung witches, and banished Quakers, we seem to have come upon halcyon days, when the once-troubled waters are calm indeed. It is indeed a pitiful case when the Christianity of to-day must rest its defense upon the more outrageous conduct of yesterday; but such a mode of argument is made legitimate by the fact that all the confidence and hope we enjoy in human affairs at large is, for the most part, founded not upon the fact of perfection, but the fact of progress. If politics should to-day attempt to read its own worth, it would not dare compare itself with the ideal of a golden future, but with the dark facts of yesterday, and would say, "Where, yesterday, you saw a cruel despotism, to-day you see a republic; where, yesterday, you heard the slave chains, to-day you hear the universal shout of liberty." But this liberty is not ideal. It is very imperfect; but you read its relative value in the groans and ignorance and inexpressible wrongs of the last generation. Thus the present, in all the non-religious divisions of its life, sees its face in the mirror of the past; and hence, when the Church would see itself, or would argue in its own defense, it is authorized to appeal to its own painful history, and then say, "I have made some progress; I have drawn a little nearer to charity, to wisdom, to truth, to God." When it comes to comparing any existing moral agency with the ideal, it will at once be seen that the Christian Church stands no further away from a perfect church than the newspaper stands away from an ideal newspaper, or our Government stands away from an ideal Republic or State. The model church, or the model Christian, is no more definitely marked out in the New Testament than the ideal journal, or senator, or state is portrayed in the intellect of mankind, and hence over all these shapes of human being there must be written one common apology: "We do not claim perfection; we claim only progress." Such is the spirit with which we must all draw near to any existing moral attribute or agency of society with the desire justly to measure its worth.

It must also be remembered that whatever idea becomes incorporated into society, and becomes a part of its daily association and life, must assume the image, not of the inventor or revealer of the idea, but of the holder of the idea at second hand. Hence marriage, a divine idea in the outset, cut loose from its divine moorings and becoming concrete in man, becomes henceforth an image of, not a divine, but of human life, and puts on the quarrels, the jealousies, the infirmities of mankind; and the ideal husband passes over a long varying scale between perfection and a tyrant, and the bride is to be found somewhere in the long path between the beautiful Eve and the unhappy Xantippe. The moment an idea, however divine, passes into the life of man, it must return to its divine beauty only so fast as man himself, in all his faculties, rises in the scale of being. Such a divine idea is the Church; and hence, entering the bosom of man, if man is a disputant by nature and wages incessant warfare with his tongue, in senate, in medicine, in law, in politics, then in theology also will the great debate continue, in a coarseness or a sweetness, according to the distance of the age or the individual from the ideal in Jesus Christ. The grand duty which lies equally before State and Church, citizen and husband, Christian and editor, is daily to struggle away from the natural man up toward the ideal stature of his peculiar world, and in this struggle we have no hesitation in saying that the Christian Church has reformed its creed and life and manners as rapidly as the bar has reformed its laws, or medicine its theories, or home its customs, or government its liberty. In the events of the present, in the turmoil of the Churches, in the calm discussions

9

and in the outbursts of half-civilized passion, I see only what one may see in the senate, or in the editorial columns of the daily papers, the onward march of a human family which neither in Church nor in editorial sanctum, nor in politics, nor in the market-place, has wholly escaped yet from the infirmities of children, or from the Pauline conception of the wild natural man. So long as the human mind possesses egotism or narrowness; so long as the heart loves self more than mankind, so long as *meum* is so loved and *tuum* is so despised or envied, so long will these infirmities of soul break forth, almost equally, in our homes, our streets, our professions, our social life and our religions; so that the final peace and glory of theology need not be expected to come by the answer which debate will ever bring all questions, but by the culture which an actual imitation of Christ will finally bring to the heart. This turmoil in religious affairs which now rages, is, we conclude, only the human heart acting as savage rather than as divine, and acting in religion just as in science or politics.

But let us return to our chief apology that the Church, in the face of all this strife, does advance both in the quality of its doctrines and as to the diminished quantity and better quality of its warfare. What a great progress in doctrine within almost the memory of the oldest of you. The last half century has by itself alone transformed the idea of God from that of an infinite, pitiless force into almost the Father and Savior of the New Testament. Reimarus in the first of our century said: "For the most part men go to perdition, and hardly one in a thousand is saved." And a venerable, pious man of the same period said: "That as in a hive of bees only one, among the many thousands, has the happiness to be queen, so with men, only one soul is saved to thousands doomed to the flames of hell." These words indicate, we may suppose, the most common belief of past times in the Church, for in harmony with such a sentiment the Augsburg confession says: "We condemn the Anabaptists who assert that unbaptized children can be saved."

But there is no demand for such a recounting of the religious atrocities of former generations. You all know enough of them to justify the conclusion that our century has almost *en masse* marched away from the great gloom, disgraceful alike to God and to the reasoning powers of His children. In the estimate made of this life, in thankfulness to God for it, in the effort to develop it in its varied paths of industry, art, love, liberty, this century is a great progress over the days when religion was only a lamentation, and when the most ashes and poverty was always the most piety.

The worthlessness of this life was so generally confessed, and even gloried in, that Calvin himself was swept along with the dust-covered monks, and from similar gloom cried out: "Earth is a place of exile. Only because God has placed us in this world we must perform our functions. It is solely the divine command which imparts a true value to our vocations. In themselves they are devoid of such." That is, no work, no social life, no books, no pleasure is of any value. We must do all things as a slave obeys his master. That the Church has escaped from this suicide of mind and heart, that it has moved away from this philosophy so unworthy of being called human, much less an inspired word, is fully attested by the intimate friendship, to-day, between Christianity and industry and science and art, and by the joy of our children, who wreathe their church-rooms with festoons, and worship their Savior, not with despair, but with joy and gratitude.

Thus confessing the shortcomings of the present Church universal, we may perceive that it is advancing as rapidly as any of its sister philosophies, politics or professional science; and is held back, not by internal falsehood or intrinsic worthlessness, but by the same defects of humanity which often make the law a doubtful profession, and turn politics, one of the noblest human pursuits, into an industry which noble minds feel, in generations here and there, called upon by self-respect to avoid. But amid all this ebb and flow of human culture and savagery, the intrinsic value of the Church remains unchanged, just as the worth of human freedom is not affected, although the streets of Paris may, in some hour of madness, in the same moment ring with the shout of freedom and drip with innocent blood. All the dear objects of earth must wait not for more truth only, but for a development of good manners.

Let us pass now to a view of this religious turmoil from another standpoint. Does all this warfare of words come from the simple "incompatibility of temper" existing in the lower forms of the human family? Oh, no! A vast quantity of it coming up from the wickedness and semi-barbarism of individual hearts, and much coming from ignorant, literal interpretations of the Bible, there yet remains a great ocean out of which the clouds of mental conflict have rolled upward in the past thousands of years, and, in the present, outward still marches this long, solemn cloud. Be men ever so honest, ever so charitable, ever so loving, coming to their pulpits, or to their counting-desks, and there attempting to express Christianity or speak of it, conflicting words will fall. The reason of this is found in the simple fact that it is demonstrative evidence alone which secures uniformity of belief, and hence any religion, any science, any theory, based not upon such demonstrative evidence, must advance through the world accompanied by the tumult of debate. Any proposition based upon thousands of variable premises or facts, based upon experiment in part, as medicine, or upon reason and experiment, as politics, will never escape conflicting opinions unless you can conceive of a distant day when every possible experiment shall have been tried and correctly reported, and that upon these experiments the mind shall act, destitute of bias, and clothed with adequate power. Thus it would seem that the hope is poor, for a day, when the physicians who stand by the bedside of the sick, and when the men who meet in Congress, shall be strangers to all variation of opinion, and shall act in silence, the great storm of ten thousand years having become a peace. Now, among those theories whose evidence is not demonstrative, but only cumulative and partial, Christianity, and religion at large, are at once seen to be classed. It has pleased God not only to enwrap with clouds the science which might cure the sick loved ones — not only the science which might make a country happy in its laws and customs — but, "clouds and darkness are about Him" in that most sacred, most solemn silence which speaks of the soul here and hereafter. Here the shadow which has fallen across all human paths toward the truth, has fallen also; and as the physician looks down upon the sick child, and knows not what to do next, stands baffled before the mystery of life and death, so the human heart, coming up to the word "religion," or "soul," is made of peculiar clay if it does not bow in a half silence, and divide its moments equally between arguments and tears. When our daily papers ridicule the Churches because they send forth conflicting voices, this ridicule must be based in part upon a forgetfulness of the fact that these journals have themselves contended for a generation, and have not yet defined and fixed a single great political truth so that it can now be removed from the arena of debate. Have they been any more successful in interpreting the constitution than the clergy have in interpreting their Scriptures? Have they learned the length and breadth of suffrage any more exactly than the sects have learned the mode and extent of salvation? Have they in a hundred years learned whether our Government has a religious quality, and may teach religion in State schools? or whether it has only the functions of a temporal machine, without a God, or an assumption of a soul? With a full consciousness of the fact that the question of women's political right was before Plato's mind two thousand years ago, and is now tossed about in the public press with no hope of finding a demonstrative answer, and knowing that it is only one of an army of such indeterminate inquiries, we feel that the religious debate should be pardoned by those men who in the great political sea have "toiled all night,"—and a long night it has been—and have caught nothing. If our able statesmen, with the written Constitution before them, have thus far been unable to determine whether the document permits or forbids the system of national banks, why is it such a shameful phenomenon when clergymen differ about the word "atonement," or signification of the word "everlasting," or the word "inspiration" itself?

It is full time that the great religious debate should receive at the hands of men in public places the palliation and perfect pardon to be found in the two facts: (1) that man is quarrelsome along all paths, (2) that there is no positive conclusion, and hence no end to debate, in realms where the evidence is not mathematical, but only approximative. While the outside scholars and critics should confess these two corollaries deduced easily from human life, those persons who stand inside the Church should doubtless be influenced by the same facts, and examine well whether their zeal for their orthodoxy is daily springing from their advanced culture and from their desire to be Christlike, or whether it comes from that half-innocent, half-civilized egotism which hates all things but self, and often with a strange pantheism identifies the "Ego" with the Almighty. In his powerful address before the Evangelical Alliance, upon the question, "How best to meet the modern infidel," Theodor Christlieb says: "We must ask him to confess that the proofs of religion are not mathematical, but only moral, and hence will not compel assent aside from the help of the moral feelings." Yes, this is the concession which the skeptical and infidel ought cheerfully to make, but these "clouds and this darkness round about God" indicate a line of conduct for the Church as for the world; for if the infidel must approach the Church sympathizing with its form of evidence, the Church must approach him not with a dogmatism and a rudeness, but with a confession that it walks by faith rather than by sight, and with a parallel confession of sorrow that it has not some proof that would carry the infidel heart over at once to the blessed land of belief and hope and peace. If the infidel must be asked to confess that there are clouds about our path and destiny, let us not ourselves set forth to meet him as from a full blaze of infinite information, but from the tenderness and humility of the same mystery with which we would envelop his heart.

The text does not leave the human family wholly

to the mercy of "clouds and darkness." There is a part of the great sky open, and thither turning, the eye may always see clear blue enough and bright stars enough to reveal the path through time's ocean and delight the heart. "Righteousness and judgment are the habitation of His throne." We know not what nor where is our God, our heaven. Around hundreds of divine ideas clouds, more or less light or heavy, roll, but the throne of God will always be found in righteousness and justice if haply any heart shall seek for it there. The soul reposing in perfect righteousness is close by the throne of his Maker and Redeemer; and that one evident fact should speak peace to the soul, and make it say of life's mysteries, "All the days of my appointed time will I wait till my change come."

Looking from these days of discordant thought into the future, we may be wholly unable to discern a golden age in which there will be no difference of opinion within the boundaries of religious thought; and it is questionable whether such an age would be golden, but if there ever shall come a time when the world shall confess the throne of God to be in "righteousness," there, in a human heart educated out of its selfishness and bitterness; there, in a society where righteousness shall have become a positive refinement of soul, (the only perfect escape from man's primitive barbarism,) the variations of religious opinion will indeed continue, but the debate will no longer be a storm full of lightnings and wrath, but a bright morning sky, full of variety of scene and sound, but equally full of peace. Toward this noble destiny of man, which each generation reveals as being nearer, I expect not so much aid to come from the noise of orthodox intellects as from the almost divine power of orthodox hearts. There of course is such a thing as Christian doctrine, but the world will draw the most of its final triumph from Christian good manners, and blessed will be the age when he will be the heterodox man who has in his heart any selfishness, or uncharity, or primeval violence. The final peace of society is to come not by the path of Christian theology, but by the more flowery path of Christian love and Christian good manners. It must become a public doctrine, and a deep feeling that he is the true betrayer of the world's Christ who wanders from Him in the deeds and in the color of his daily life. When the Christian world shall thus interpret Jesus, as a form of being, the rudeness of the great debate will have passed away. Infidels that could not be driven shall be more gently won, and the clouds and darkness of the moral argument will weigh little against mortals who are following that path of righteousness upon which alone a perpetual sunlight falls.

CHARLES SUMNER.

SERMON VIII.

CHARLES SUMNER.

"The powers that be are ordained of God."

THE world has always loved to speak of the Infinite One as being the "God of Nations," because there is a greatness involved in the idea of Nation which makes it seem worthy of the attention and love of the Infinite. It is easy for the individual heart, possessed of ordinary humility, to feel quite overlooked in the daily administrations of Providence, but a nation is something so vast in its interests and in its life which lies over centuries, that into its great events men can generally see descending, in love or wrath, the sublime form of God. Notwithstanding the most elaborate and conclusive argument that our Heavenly Father is in all places and times alike, yet we all go away from the argument to confess Him sooner at Waterloo than where a child is playing or a bird singing; more visible where slaves are shouting in a new liberty than where the farmer turns his furrow or the lonely woodman swings his axe. Thus marking the habits of the human mind, we may perceive at least how great a thing is a nation. What a vast idea it is, that it always claims the care of the Almighty, and almost compels the atheist to confess that there is at least a nation's God.

A nation is a second world into which we are all born. The first world is only the good green earth, with its seasons, and food, and labor, and natural vicissitudes; but this is a poor birth-place for a mind or a soul; for into these poor, brutish arms falls the Indian child or the young Arab. To be born into earth alone is a fate that robs a birthday of all worth. It is only an animal that is born to earth alone. It is only when some second world called a "nation" becomes the soul's cradle that it becomes desirable to fall heir to life. A nation is a grand equipment for a career; it is food, and clothes, and friends first, and education, and employment, and culture, and religion afterward. It is the atmosphere into which the many-winged spirit comes; and a bird might as well spread its wings in a vacuum as for a human soul to be born away from the treasured-up virtues of a national life. When the rude black face, with retreating fore-head and great thick lips, meets you on the Southern coast, you know that being was born, but you associate with this knowledge the other fact that he was born to savage Africa. Great beyond all estimate, therefore, is the fact of *nation*, for it shapes the soul, and is the joy or sorrow of every being that comes into this existence. As when, in the setting sun, after a summer shower, all things, clouds, hills, trees, and even the very grass and the faces of our friends standing in the refracted light are covered with the tinge of gold, so when man is born into a nation he is instantly bathed in its light, and sets forth in a double destiny, that of man and that of citizen; and it is, for the most part, the latter destiny that determines the value of life. When Bunyan saw a culprit ascending the steps to the gallows, he said: "That were I but for the Grace of God;" but this Grace does not busy itself only with individuals here and there, but it marks out a vast realm and makes it a great, free, civilized state, and then the millions that come into life in its blessed confines can, in their later years, when they realize the value of the great fatherland, say, "I was a savage, a Congo negro, but for the Grace of God." Next to the grandeur of a planet that carries a thousand millions of people upon its bosom, and whirls them along through day and night, and summer and winter, and youth and old age, comes the grandeur of a well-equipped State which, for hundreds of years, guards the liberty, and industry, and education, and happiness of its dependent millions, crowding its influence in upon them gently as the atmosphere lies upon the cheek in June. Her language, her peculiar genius, her ideals, her religion, her freedom, enwrap us better than our mother's arms, for the State enwraps her too, and wreaths her forehead with a merit that warrants her office and her affection. The State is defined to be a

> * * Sovereign law, that with collected will,
> Sits Empress, crowning good, repressing ill.
> Smit by her sacred frown
> The fiend dissension like a vapor sinks
> And e'en the all dazzling crown
> Hides his faint rays and at her bidding shrinks.

Whence comes this grand instrument which, as now existing in our continent, under the flag of liberty, pours around forty millions of people such a golden air as no millions ever breathed before? Who gathered these flowers that wreathe equally our cradle, our altar, our homes, and our whole earthly pilgrimage? This much of a reply is given by human experience: Nothing comes to man, of excellence, without labor. All that man possesses of art, or science, or literature, or invention, has come by regular payments made in hard toil. As the verdure that waves over the whole earth has come from the daily sacrifice of the sun's heat, so the glory manifold of each great nation has come by the path of human sacrifice of thought, and toil, and even life; and so valuable have been the national ideas, that, for all the good the world possesses, there have been fields baptized with the heart's best blood. Young though many of the modern free nations may be in their present name and form, yet, back of each one lie a thousand years of active labor, and often of deep agony. As geologists now tell us that before God fitted up this earth for man, while the mists were rising from its heated seas, and condensing in the cooler upper air, there were often awful storms where the thunder rolled incessantly for a hundred years; so each nation which we see standing forth now in peace and beauty — England, Germany, America — has emerged from a thousand-year storm, where the wrath of man has rolled in thunder for centuries, and the cruel skies have rained blood. One of the poets says:

> "A thousand years scarce serve to form a state.'

And oh! what years of toil and vicissitude they are to the brains which stand at the throne, and to the hearts that stand in the battle, and to the widow and orphan which weep when the smoke rolls away and reveals the dead.

If then a great nation like our own has come over a two-thousand-year path under a sky of alternate peace and storm, come along from free Athens, and free Rome and sacred Palestine, there must have been all along guardian angels of its long journey, glorious leaders of its wilderness march; souls that smote rocks for its thirsty multitudes, and prayed down manna in the still night. The morals of our day can look back and see their Seneca, their Confucius, but chiefly their Divine Jesus; the art of our era looks back and beholds its Phidias, its Apelles, its Angelo, linking the future and the past; poetry and all literature look back and cast smiles of gratitude to Homer and Thucydides and Dante; the law confesses the deep devotion of Cicero and Justinian as minds who studied justice when the world seemed young; and now, beholding this differentiation of men by a wise providence of God, so that each part of the soul's vast vineyard may have some one to love its vines, we reach the easy conclusion that the same wisdom will permit us always to hold in memory and in love men who, turning aside from other pursuits, have found in the study and love and service of their nation their own special path between the cradle and the grave. It is a blessed thought that there have risen up here and there hearts not only that could weave the sweet songs of a Virgil, and not only hands that could paint the pictures of a Parrhasius, or that could strike the notes of a Mozart; not only minds that may throw up a dome of St. Peter's, or that may astonish the world with their invention, but also other hearts which have loved the idea of nation, and have lived and died not in the arms of a friend, but rather in the arms of the country. Out of the thoughts and love and specialization of these great ones we, humbler children of the State, have all drawn our happiness and freedom, as the violets are invited into life by the all-loving sun.

In the week past the grave has opened suddenly and taken back one of these souls which seem sent of God to know nothing else but their country, as Paul knew nothing else but the Cross. Into that tomb which grows wider each year and has received away from our sight Washington and the Adamses and Jefferson and Clay and Webster and Lincoln, at last has been gathered one more name wreathed as heavily as any with the glorious ideas and honors of our great Republic. Napoleon loved not a nation, but his own power. He was not a student of justice, but of crowns; he studied how to destroy other diadems, and of their jewels weave one for himself.

The triumph and the vanity
The rapture of the strife,
The earthquake voice of victory,
To thee the breath of life;
The sword, the scepter, and that sway,
Which man seemed made but to obey,
Wherewith renown was rife,
All quell'd! Dark Spirit, what must be
The madness of thy memory!

But the memory of that life just ended has no madness in it, but is all a remembrance of honor, and charity, and peace.

It seems especially fitting the day and place that we should devote this hour to thoughts over this fresh tomb, for the greatness of Mr. Sumner's career is strangely interwoven with some of the noblest ideas of Christianity; and this union was not accidental, nor prudential, but spiritual and intellectual, for Mr. Sumner in his life, devoted to humanity, so framed all his arguments, and so based them upon the philosophy of Christ that the perpetual return of the terms Christianity and Savior betrays the fact that much of his eloquence was only the Sermon upon the Mount applied, not to the future of the soul, but to the true, earthly progress of mankind. If any group of philosophers were to sit down with the Life of Christ in their hands, with the desire to elaborate a political constitution from its pages, among the many principles they would bring forth we should at once certainly find these—peace, justice, and equality. From justice would instantly come liberty. Now of that eventful life whose untimely ending drapes this day with sorrow, these three Christian ideas, peace, liberty, and equality, were the opening and final strain, the matin and the vesper. The public career of Mr. Sumner began by that unrivaled oration spoken thirty years ago upon peace as the source of national grandeur; and without any deviation, any faltering along this path, he is found at last on the border of death, asking Congress not to paint upon its flags of the present and future the names of battles where brothers fought. His life was all set to one music, and it was a heavenly strain without discord.

But before I ask you to think of those three great ideas, in which Mr. Sumner did great service for the Christianity out of which he took the ideas, and the Christlike spirit, too, permit me to apologize, so far as it may be necessary, for the marble coldness which has long been associated with this eminent character. Let us empty our minds of this prejudice. A public man, writing a private letter since the death of this senator, says: "He was cold as a statue. He was a child of principles and books, and consequently had little in common with the humanities of life. * * *

I cannot speak of him generally in this regard; but in the few times in which I dined with him at Mr. Lincoln's table, he was a pleasant dinner companion, and conversed happily and instructively; but such times were only little outbreaks of sunlight. In the main, he was behind the cloud, and, while full of gentle humanity, he moved among individuals evolving an austere sense of superiority." Against the truth of these statements from one who had the opportunity and the discrimination for reading well the qualities of this distinguished man, we would say nothing; indeed, the portraiture just given may be confessed to be sufficiently correct. But that he was capable of deep friendship is fully seen in his attachment to the loved President, whose house was so dear to him that he repaired there daily as to a sacred home where he loved all and was also deeply loved. Passing by this inquiry, I only wish to remind you that all the great intellectual development which the world has ever seen has been reached at the cost of the heart. "Where the treasure is," says the Bible, "there the heart will be also"; and hence, when an old scholar of the dark ages found his love of thought increasing, he began to withdraw from the streets, and to find, in some monastic cell, all of the world that any longer remained in his heart; and although the dark ages are gone, and the monasteries are dust, yet the principle remains that, when the intellect weds itself fully to certain paths of study and toil, the heart soon sunders the other many sweet and beautiful associations of the wide world, and casts its love upon that realm only to which the intellect may have wedded itself for better or for worse, for richer or poorer. It is an unconscious sacrifice which genius is always compelled to make; but it is no more visible over the grave of Sumner than over the grave of Mill in philosophy, or Pascal in metaphysics, or Angelo in art, or Cicero in law and letters. It is written in all history that a life of thought is a constant warfare against a life of sociability and cheerfulness and love. Instead of recalling the marble coldness of past illustrious men as a blemish or a fault in their character, we only indicate a common fact, and we would bury the defect forever under offerings of gratitude, that there have come here and there souls which, for the development of great, useful ideas, have been able to abandon what we mortals in a humbler vale call the varied pleasures of life. But they have not so much lost happiness as exchanged that of sense for that of spirit. Turning aside now from this apology, let us rejoice that if it was the fate of the lamented senator to live for only a part of earth and for only a part of religion, that it pleased him to live for so magnificent a part of both politics and religion as is found in the words peace, justice, and liberty.

It was not Mr. Sumner, you remember, who advised the partnership of bibles and rifles in the early days of Kansas. No, in all this forty years of public life, Mr. Sumner stood by the power of argument, of light, of Christian civilization alone. His hymn was the poet's psalm of peace:

Were half the power that fills the world with terror,
 Were half the wealth bestowed on camps and courts,
Given to redeem the human mind from error,
 There were no need of arsenals or forts.

The warrior's name would be a name abhorred,
 And every nation that should lift again
Its hand against a brother, on its forehead
 Would wear, forever more, the curse of Cain.

In the pulpits of the whole land the gospel doctrines had, for the most part, been applied to only individual welfare, and chiefly to that welfare beyond the confines of states — beyond the grave. Afraid, for the most part, to preach what they called politics; and having, to an alarming extent, such a bad politics that it was perhaps fortunate that they remained silent even by a theological mistake, the Christian ministry had, in the last generations, left the gospel of nations to be preached by the few disciples of William Penn and by such virtual Quakers as Channing and Whittier, and Sumner, the greatest of all. Upon him there was no restraint. No false creed, no temporary policy such as influenced Webster and Clay, no fear of violence, no fear of public scorn, either from Boston or New Orleans, ever held him in any conceivable chain, but from him, the freest man our country ever had in its dark days, came the gospel of nations in all its Bethlehem beauty of truth and spirit. In the present, and more yet, in the near and far future, the pulpit will confess that Charles Sumner was a minister at its altar in dark days when it was afraid, and in doctrines to the grandeur of which it had not the intellect, nor the courage, nor the humanity to ascend. Penn and Channing and Sumner came in with that part of Christianity which belongs to the constitution of nations; and when we remember that a grand, free, enlightened State is the land in which the Cross can ever be reared with most success, the orators who, upon the field of statesmanship, apply to society the three Christian doctrines of peace, liberty and justice, must be confessed to be standing very near the holiest ministers of religion. As the church helped Mr. Sumner, gave him hearts willing to listen to his long argument, so he helped the church by sending back to it men who evermore tried to combine the character of Christian with the character of citizen.

But Mr. Sumner's attachment to peace was no more absorbing and unbending than his devotion to liberty. But liberty is twin sister of peace, as bondage is the companion of violence. As Franklin gloried in saying "Where liberty is there is my country," Sumner equally gloried in saying "Where liberty is there is my party." Down this channel of freedom, for white slaves in Barbary, and for black slaves in America, he poured a torrent of eloquence for twenty-five years, a stream of argument, which gathering up the wisdom of Greece and Rome, the experience of England, the battle-shouts of Marathon and Bunker Hill, the blest vision of all the poets, the longings of Washington and Jefferson, and then bedecking the stream with flowers of a gorgeous rhetoric growing upon either bank, moved along like an Amazon toward the sea. It has been said recently by a public man, that Mr. Sumner "surpassed all statesmen in the love and study of the right." It was this deep prepossession that led him to espouse the cause of the slave. Words which he himself applied to Channing thirty years ago return now to settle upon his own forehead. "Follow my white plume," said the chivalrous monarch of France. Follow the right, more resplendent than plume or oriflamme, was the watchword of Sumner. But all this long history you know well, for in this hour when death has come to quicken our memory and love, an hour which makes an enemy a friend, all that past struggle for the slave's freedom, and the discord of the Missouri compromise down to the death of Mr. Lincoln, a tragedy which closed the long, awful drama, flashes through your hearts with no detail of sadness left out. Recall the great pageant and see this white face above the common mortals.

But to-day, we can only turn aside from the usual themes of the sacred desk to bless the Heavenly Father for this child that came in the name of that form of civilization which finds its best exponent in the Savior of mankind, and bless him that there was one tongue which, for a generation, made the best eloquence of this free land beam with the light of Him whose gospel is not only a perfect salvation, but a perfect civilization, — the vital air, not only of a saint, but of a citizen. But we cannot close these thoughts without asking you to read in this urn of perishable dust, but of imperishable memory, a lesson of hope which may serve us all in coming days, perhaps of the country, but surely of our own heart. When government, and pulpit, and press were voiceless and hopeless as to a time when the nation's flag should be freed from its last reproach, this mental sight which is closed now saw plainly in the future a day when all the States would be free, and when the national banner would proclaim liberty and justice wherever it should wave. His was a hopefulness which nothing but death could abate; and blest with such a prophetic, almost inspired sense, he, in all the years of our civil war, was calm, and was to Mr. Lincoln, upon whose mind and heart a burden rested which would have wearied an Atlas accustomed to uphold the globe, a daily messenger of faith and hope in both man and God. Perhaps the marble-like nature of the statesman was a peace and strength to a president whose heart was always full of tenderness and melancholy strangely mingled. That immense power of hope which has always attended men of ideals, the angel of their need, accompanied Mr. Sumner in all hours, and held him up far above the discord of the passing time. A poem which he greatly loved shows us what kind of a hymn sounded in the sky over his daily toil. It inspired him in the night watches:

"There's a fount about to stream,
There's a light about to beam,
There's a warmth about to glow,
There's a flower about to blow.
There's a midnight blackness changing
Into gray;
Men of thought and men of action
Clear the way!"

Oh! why may not the pulpit and each Christian rise to this calm atmosphere of a trust in God, and as this statesman always saw liberty and justice about to come down out of God's sky, why may not the soldier of the cross daily say to his soul

> "There is a fount about to stream,
> There is a light about to beam,"

and live in this magnificent hope?

But our time has passed. Much of our country's mental and moral glory has gone down in past years. We seem to have only an evening horizon into which golden suns sink, but from which none arise. The melancholy gate of death by which these souls depart seems wider than the gates of life by which such glorious beings are marching toward our bereaved hearts. But this apparent triumph of the grave may come from the fact that we can see the past in all its desolation, but cannot unveil the future and see its compensating good. We can only hope that the gates of God's mercy are as wide as the gates of His death, and that the solemn West into which these lights are sinking from our sky, may, by its shadows, remind us that there is an Eastern heavens radiant with divine love, upon whose bosom other orbs will appear resplendent with peace, justice, and liberty.

THE LOST PARADISE.

SERMON IX.

THE LOST PARADISE.

"So He drove out the man, and He placed at the east of the garden of Eden cherubim, and a flaming sword which turned every way, to keep the way of the tree of life."—*Genesis 3:24.*

THE Biblical history of man's first days upon earth is a most wonderful symbol of all the subsequent history of mankind. That honor and that dishonor, that happiness and that sorrow, seem a microscopic photograph of the coming world, whose nine hundred millions of people in two hemispheres were to find and lose honor; and find and lose happiness daily for thousands of years. As there is an art which can copy the great London newspaper upon a space not larger than a child's finger-nail, as all the long columns of markets and of daily events, and of speeches of members of parliament, retreat into that minute image without loss of letter or even minutest mark of punctuation, so the vast history of the human family, coming in from old Asia or New America, flying back from the days of Solomon, or Cæsar, or Napoleon, betakes itself into this first picture of man, and finds there a perfect image of all its joy and grief and of the causes producing them. In one of the Arabian stories a sight-seer beheld a long, bright cloud, which, like a column of smoke from a volcano, reaching out over the sea, began to withdraw, and watching it he saw it hide itself all away in a copper vase on the beach, a vase which a fisherman could have carried in one hand to his hut. Whoever looks out upon the great outspread human race, and then looks at this first of Genesis, will seem to have found an urn containing all of human life and death, greatness and weakness. Subsequent centuries have been only the enlargement of the picture. Paradises innumerable have come and gone; Adams and Eves many have one day been happy and the next day been exiles, and always for the same reason, a disregard of divine law.

Before we look at some of these mirrored causes of human failure and success, let us recall to mind what a large part of this story of the garden of Eden must be true even if it made no pretense to being an inspired narrative. It is not, certainly, a myth that there is a human race; and hence, there must have been a first pair in this long series, and this first pair must have had a first home and a Creator just at hand; and this pair must have made their first move in virtue or sin; and from what sin we now see in the world, not much doubt can remain as to what line of conduct this first pair followed, and that they early left a paradise of virtue is the verdict of history. The theory most in conflict with this Bible picture of primitive man is the almost popular notion that man is a gradual result of progress in the animal kingdom, and never had a paradise, but is on the way toward one, from a cellular and electric starting-point a million years back. Against this theory, however, rises up the fact that in the thousands of years of history no animal is showing the least sign of passing over into that moral consciousness, that selfhood which so wonderfully distinguishes man. The highest order of brutes are doing absolutely nothing toward forming a language or toward reaching that consciousness of "me" and "not me," which joins man to the Divine; there is no effort visible on the part of the most intelligent *quadrumana* to build a school-house or start a country newspaper; and if in the historic period no progress whatever has been made, and that too with the advantage of human association, what could they have done in two historic periods? If six thousand years give *nothing*, what will six million years give? The best reason I can myself bring to bear upon this matter leads me to see man setting forth as man, and setting forth from a Creator; hence he had a place which we may call Eden, and easily reason may join the Bible in giving it river banks and trees and flowers and the song of birds.

Let us now in imagination visit this primitive man in his Selkirk loneliness, and find what there was in his situation which explains the loss of that Eden, and the loss of so many blessed homes since that early banishment. I shall not try to gather up all the facts of the case, for this would involve a discussion of free-will, and of the relation of a perfect God to the fact of evil in his world. We must omit much, also, of the poetic meditation our century might weave over that little era. Let me ask you to notice only one fact in the surroundings of original man, the fact that he was ordered to live a restricted life, and must not expect to be as boundless as God. The situation we may suppose to be expressed in these words: "Thou, oh man, mayest claim a grand, large world, but it shall not be infinite; there is a tree of which thou shalt not eat; between thee and perfect absolutism a great dividing ocean must always roll. Thy world shall not be the whole universe, but only a continent. Thy power, thy ambition, thy knowledge, shall be within banks — beautiful banks, indeed, with sunshine and flowers, but still, boundaries to check thy stream." Such was the situation, indeed, for we read it no longer in Genesis alone, but in subsequent facts which have removed the picture from the danger of mythology, and have stereotyped it in all history. This law of limitation man did not respect, but declared himself to be monarch of all; and soon afterward he found himself an exile, and a flaming sword waving between him and the tree of life—between him and the absolutism of God. This is the event which history has taken up and verified, not only in nations but in almost each individual heart; and out of this long history comes to us to-day, in loud accents, the announcement of a great principle, that human life is a *restricted* life, a life subject to law, and that he who confesses this subjection remains in Eden, he who denies it is banished. The antiquarians are seeking the place where the first Eden must have been; but while they thus seek, let us behold in all the ruins between Babylon and Rome places where the gates of happiness have been closed only because the inmates of the garden declined to accept a world limited by any law or presence of God, but daily hurled their free-will along as though the human heart were the only deity. Just as the body will flourish only under its limited quantity of labor, or food, or pain, or pleasure, so the soul is encompassed by its peculiar laws, and all its development and happiness lie within those God-made walls, and the hour that sees man reaching his hand for fruits beyond these walls, sees the flaming sword drawn between by the hand of the Invisible. The human soul was filled with a group of virtues, but each one of these was marked with its confines, beyond which was grief. Each virtue had its own forbidden tree. Take any one; for example, ambition. By its powerful stimulus, society has been carried along to success and happiness. The eloquence of old statesmen from Pericles to Burke, the sweetness of poetry from Sappho to Bryant, the beauty of art from Phidias to Angelo, the struggles for liberty from the Hebrew slaves to the American colonies, have all come in part from the sentiment of ambition which has everywhere filled the soul with nobleness, and has redoubled its power and desire to escape degradation, and rise up to a holier region of being and action. Before all minds there is an ideal excellence in the department of their special industry. The world despises the one who has not the ambition to seek the better thing along his path. We all scorn the heart that has no noble impulse. Having now found this tree of which one may eat, and of which all noble souls have eaten, we immediately perceive that God has placed restrictions in this garden, and has said there is one tree of which you may not eat. This ambition must flow within a limited channel. It must be clothed with humility; not with the vanity of an Alexander; not with the presumption of a Herod, who desired to be called a god; not with the insane hungering of Cardinal Wolsey, who wept forth, "Fling away ambition; by that sin fell the angels"—for the instant this sentiment passes the confines of the most tender justice toward others, or begins to make the heart aspire toward the throne of the Almighty, the paradise all dissolves, and no researches can, after a time, find any traces of the Eden which this heart possessed before the "vaulting ambition" had "overleaped itself." Literature is full of praise of this sentiment in its young, sweet days, and equally full of sad requiems over the grave of its final dishonor. Shakspeare says, "Who soars too near the sun with golden wings, melts them." Another says this "ambition is the mind's immodesty." Byron says, "Blood is valuable to wash ambition's hands;" and you all remember now the familiar line:

"The path of glory leads but to the grave."

It may be singular that in the same garden there may be trees of which all may eat, and then near by, growing in the same soil, a tree, of which eating, thou shalt surely die; but such is the world into which we are born, and the boundary having been crossed, light begins to fade, the rose turns into a thorn, the vine into a thistle, and the heart that was happy yesterday to-day "eats its bread in the sweat of the face." At night the soul's dew is only bitter tears. We have all seen this sentiment (and I use it only to illustrate a whole class) feeding upon the heart and soul of statesmen, leading them away from study, from wisdom, from honor, and from all happiness, and finally, as Lilly says, it knows but two steps, one down to blood or another up only so far as envy. Thus the very hands which are appointed of the Creator to build up a paradise stand ever ready to pull it down again if a given boundary is passed. The love of money is a lawful, most wise sentiment. There are few scenes more charming than that of an industrious man acquiring each year property which may help him to contentment or may furnish the table of his children, and stand between them and beggary and hardship and vice. This love of gold, rising up with civilization, is a cause of human progress. It is therefore a paradise builder, but just by it is a tree of which you may not eat. It is a tree of life and death with you, and eating of it the face whitens, the features harden, the heart shrivels, and *miser* (the miserable) is written upon the brow, the worst curse-mark from mankind or God. It is almost an occupation of a year to look over literature to learn what terms it has tried to find worthy of application to so wretched a member of society. Even old Publius said: "The miser is remarkable in that he wants what he already has." Another says: "A miser's life is an act at which we applaud only the closing scene." But this wretched mortal is only a sentiment which has in a brief time traveled from a paradise to a hell. It is man out of his boundary.

Thus it appears that the foundation stone of human life is that of *obedience to law.* God only is absolute. He graciously fashioned a life apart from Himself. He crowned it with His image, a shadow of Himself; but as He made the ocean to roll between shores, and said to it, "Thus far shalt thou come, and no farther, here shall thy proud wave be stayed," so He placed the created soul between banks, and said, here only may thy bright waters flow. The banks are not narrow. Human life need not be called a river, for it is vast as the ocean, deep and strong and sublime; but it has a shore all around to separate it from God, and along that shore the cherubim stand, and flaming swords gleam to banish those who cross the boundary marked all around by the finger of the Almighty. In such a limited but vast world it is easy to see what is that thing called sin. "It is a want of conformity unto, or actual transgression of, the law of God." The industrious man God loves, but the miser has taken a beautiful sentiment and transgressed it, abused it, reviled it, crucified it. The noble aspirations of the young, God loves, but the vanity of an Atilla, or a Belshazzar, or a Cæsar, or a Napoleon, where the soul cuts all the bands of justice and of humility, finds at last a lonely grave at St. Helena, or at some feast reads upon the wall the words of sudden, helpless doom, and Babylon is dust. Sin, then, is an uprising of the heart against God, it is the overflow as a stream once beautiful, saying, "I will be a river no more, I will expand into infinite space and be a law and a shore unto myself alone." If there be a secret of human well-being and real triumph, it must lie in a full appreciation of the grand breadth of life and then in a willingness to pause the instant the foot comes to a boundary of God. Years ago, when universal liberty began to be discussed in our National Congress, one distinguished speaker arose and said: "I desire to speak to-day of some laws greater than any passed in this capital or in this country, older than America, older than India,—I mean the laws of God." This was a sentence full of real eloquence. But it was true, not as to human politics alone, but as to the whole heart and mind of man. Here we all are to-day, in a wide world indeed, but on all sides, our love, our ambition, our pleasures, our action toward our fellow-men and toward self, are to act within the laws of the Almighty. As a bird can fly only within the atmosphere, and may move a thousand miles along the surface of the beautiful earth, but not far upward away from its bowers, so man may move within certain confines, but the moment he reveals any "want of conformity unto, or any transgression of, the law of God," his world is ruined in all its beauty and delicate plan.

It is wonderful that the human heart is not so thankful for the gift of life as to be perfectly willing to accept of the limitations which surround it, and being in a vast garden, with only one tree denied, and with a whole forest of sweet fruits on all sides and free, it is marvelous that we do not cheerfully accept the situation, and leave the forbidden fruit to bloom and ripen and decay untouched, undreamed of. But such is not our history, and hence earth, from the Eden of the Euphrates to the prairies of the West, is covered with the ruins of homes once full of honor and happiness. Permit me to illustrate our theme. Many years ago, a beautiful, educated lady of Sandusky grew weary of her home. It was a good earthly paradise. Her husband, her little daughter, her music, her wealth, made her home not one of public contempt, but of public admiration and envy. The poor looked at her mansion as at a land of the blest. But her heart seems not to have known that human life has boundaries, that love has its ordinary channels and is not absolute as immensity; seems not to have remembered that the bird can indeed fly sweetly, but only in its narrow atmosphere, and thus oblivious of the dividing cherubim in Eden, she fled with a high official, the collector of the city, that in the glorious tropic land amid perpetual spring and flowers, they might build up a home, not of mild contentment, but of unmingled bliss. But this poor heart in one short summer time found that happiness is a dependent plant, having its roots interwoven with other plants, and when lifted from its companions withers and dies. Leaving her little daughter in a grave among the tropic flowers, which made a happier wreath for the dead child than for the living mother, our poor exile fled with her companion to the Mauritius, hoping a still more beautiful clime might bring back the color to her face and peace to her heart. But it was not the climate nor the dead girl, that was waging war upon that cheek and heart. It was God. She had gone beyond the dividing line in Eden, and she was being expelled from paradise. Each hour the cherubim and the flaming swords were crowding between her and the blessed home of her sinless years. She started in most abject desolation of spirit to sail back for the old home, but in mid-ocean her broken heart ceased to beat, and those silent ocean depths became her tomb. Oh, what paradises are being daily lost in this reckless, thoughtless, even God-defying world! Happiness is interwoven with justice. But this lamented lady tore it from its soil and inweaving it with injustice toward her husband, her child, her friends, herself, and society, and her God, she expected it to become absolute bliss, but she found that the laws of the Almighty could not be broken, but that in this conflict it is always the heart that breaks.

It is not in this domain of love only that success is limited by a most divine and careful justice. In all business life and social life, there is a forbidden tree of which, having eaten, the soul's peace begins to die.

Not many months ago one of our own bankers disappeared. Upon a certain morning a few poor people who went to the accustomed steps to draw some fragment of their carefully gathered savings, found, to their dismay, that the doors were closed against them. The scene soon became pitiful. There, behind those doors, five hundred persons — widows, orphans, servant girls, poor workingmen, making up a large part of the multitude — had gone in months and years past to lay down with a smile of confidence and success the savings of hard toil. And the banker was, in those days, also kind and affable, and, perhaps, deeply honest. He was happy, too, but he forgot the conditions, the limitation of happiness. It escaped him that human life has around it a line like that once at the base of Sinai, to cross which is death, the soul is pierced through with a dart. And there is no department in God's world where the line of duty is so plainly marked out as in the banking part of this large Eden. Its law is this: "That which is taken in over the counter must be handed back again." Not to hand back the deposited gold is the forbidden tree. The banker, disregarding this limitation, not only the weeping widows and orphans crowd around the marble steps, but the cherubim and flaming sword of Genesis quickly rush between the banker and his paradise. Upon a certain morning, as we said, this citizen was wanting. He had no choice left but to fly from the friends of years, from his home, from a city he loved, and, above all, from the good name which he once possessed. And in this long, wordless absence has he been happy? Does the heart die that eats of the forbidden tree? Two weeks ago there came to me a letter from a distant point, not even a town, but a place where steamers touch, and where the postmark is written with a pen; and, upon opening this letter, it is a simple burst of sorrow from this cultivated, exiled, lonely and repentant man. It was never my lot to know or even meet this citizen, but in his banishment and apparent grief he has come to days when he wishes to empty his heart of so much of its bitterness as words and, no doubt, tears can take away. I give here a few words from his long letter, not only because they may help young men in coming hours when temptation may assail, but because the far-away writer of them would be perfectly willing thus to warn the young business friends he left here, and would no doubt gladly see them avoiding his method of blighting life's hope.

"With what a heart-burning and contrition I look back upon a ruined, shipwrecked life can be known only to the great Searcher of hearts. * * * I always knew what was right, but religion was with me only an intellectual conviction, not an active life within, influencing and controlling my actions, and hence when temptation came to accumulate riches, I yielded and fell, and have lost my good name; have made my family miserable, and caused distress upon a wide circle. I flattered myself that there would be time and some way to avert any calamity, and thus, between flattery and self-deception, the day of accounting came, and I woke to find the ship run into, and the water pouring in at all points. I was going to the bottom. * * * Oh, is there not some truth to be so known and seen as to be fully appreciated, and thus poured all through my spiritual life, and bending my will and feelings all beneath its folds? * * * I stand afar off and have hardly courage to lift my eyes toward God. Let me not be forgotten in your prayers. In longings for Christ, your brother. * * *"

Yes, there is a truth, of a twofold nature, able to meet this whole question of a paradise lost. The truth that God is around every individual soul with His bounding will, is one which if regarded will keep the Eden blessed so far as earth can any longer, by the path of humble obedience alone, find a spiritual peace. The citizen who, to the best of his light, humbly walks with God, is permitted to move among his fellow-men, enjoying the sweets of hope and friendship, and the esteem of society. For him there is no banishment, no bitter tears. But this truth is no longer wide enough to meet the wants of man, for he is already out of his best paradise, he is away from his God. This truth, therefore, assumes another form. We call it Jesus Christ. He came to earth to rebuild the torn down Edens of us all. We are all exiles.

Our tears might well mingle with those of the exiled banker, if he be penitent, and we may say along with him, "We stand afar off." This Christ has fulfilled a law which we have broken, and to us, no longer able to flee unto ourselves and find peace, He says, "Come unto *Me* all ye that labor and are heavy laden, and I will give you rest." At His voice, all divine, the cherubim that stand between Him and the paradise lost fall back, fall back, and lo, the exile, penitent and loving and trusting, sees the gate of joy open again, and he hears not only the angels rejoice over the sinner that repenteth, but he hears the forgiveness of his fellow-men, and the paradise that is destined to be perfect beyond this world begins now and here to cast forward some of its light, and it dries up tears and binds up broken hearts, and calls back exiles all along this side the tomb.

POSITIVE RELIGION.

SERMON X.

POSITIVE RELIGION.

"Think not that I am come to destroy the law or the prophets. I am not come to destroy but to fulfill."—*Matt. 5 : 17.*

INASMUCH as the Jewish ceremonial law was to be abolished by this Christ, and inasmuch as the state laws so far as they were cruel and unjust were also about to be set aside, the Savior must have alluded here to the moral law in its broadest sense, as being written or unwritten. He had just enumerated several of these higher laws, such as "Blessed are the pure in heart," "Blessed are those that hunger and thirst after righteousness." After enumerating quite a number of sublime principles, He said that whoever should break the least of these commandments and teach men so, should be least in the kingdom of heaven, and the converse also was stated. Thus we perceive that Christ in this great chapter had risen to an upper air far above the ceremonial law and far above those state laws that had been valuable in a particular time, but formed no part of the world's perpetual and unchanging good. Among the everlasting law. and prophets which Christ came not to destroy, He soon includes what we now call the golden rule and the law of loving even one's enemies. In a word, Christ came not as an innovator, or a disturber of the world's peace, but as the best friend of man, to set in clear light what had been standing in deep shadow. He was a progress along a path in which men were already walking, but with such slowness and such stumbling as to awaken divine pity. From this text, therefore, I shall ask you to draw the lesson of *positiveness in religion*, a lesson of warning against that unbelief which seems so popular in our day. By unbelief I do not mean that form of it which simply rejects what is called the orthodox faith, but that form of it, now prevalent, which distrusts everything hitherto grouped under the name of religion, from the being of a personal God to the doctrine of a future existence. The unbelief of Thomas Paine and Hume was chiefly against any revealed religion; but the unbelief of our day is against even a natural religion, and is little less hostile to a Christ than to a God.

Against that criticism of the present which is not a development so much as a destruction, I would love to-day to argue in favor of positivism, of fulfillment rather than of this interminable and dreary destruction of old ideas. Let us first notice that thought has its habits just as the drinking man or the opium eater, or as has the benevolent man or the warrior. When the benevolent-man walks through the streets of a city he hears every cry of distress from man or brute, and when the military soul passes along the same thoroughfare he sees soldiers in the workmen, and cavalry chargers in the horses that draw the carriages upon the avenues. But there is nothing in nature that limits habit to any one department of life. All of Nature's laws are universal, and hence that peculiar condition called habit will attach itself to the logical faculty as readily as to the appetite of the drunkard, or the gait of one who walks, or the tones and gestures of one who speaks. It will come to pass that the reasoning power will in successive periods acquire habits that will carry it beyond propriety, beyond wisdom, and make it a slave of custom rather than the wise king of society. In the age preceding our own, reason operated chiefly in the domain of the marvelous. Not having found the modern great premise that the universe is pervaded by general law, but having adopted another major premise, that God and Satan came forward each day with new and independent events of good or evil, the reason of that period busied itself in finding in what dream or in what occurrence these mysterious wonder-workers had last appeared, and what lessons were to be drawn from the miracles of yesterday or last night. The great universe of law had not yet arisen upon their intellects or hearts. Such became their habit of expecting the miraculous that all ordinary events disgusted them by their monotony, and left them longing for a daily invasion from lawless powers of the air. In such iron chains did this habit hold the past that even Luther hurled his inkstand at the devil, and Sir Matthew Hale saw old women possessed of witches which bore these aged people through the air, and made omnipresent and fiendish persons who to all common appearances were at home innocent and even gentle and affectionate. To overthrow this base of reasoning that the world was ruled by two powers, God and Satan, who invaded human life afresh each day with events without human cause, and substitute a platform of law, making the world intelligible and its causes and effects in a degree attainable or avoidable, was an immense task, for society had, in all its long career, been inwoven with and entangled among the mysteries of superstitious belief, and to escape the habit was like asking a new era to make an entirely new order of souls. But vast as the task was, it was undertaken consciously and unconsciously, and year by year visions and dreams and miracles and witches and goblins and ghosts were expelled from the only place where they ever existed — the brain of man. Look back for a moment and see what a burden of superstition had to be cut away from man's shoulders; and it was not like cutting the straps of a camel's load in the desert, but it was like removing a tumor from the brain itself. All the long way from the time when Romulus and Remus were nursed by a wolf to the time when Luther saw Satan, and when the Catholic church saw Luther's soul borne to hell by a procession of ravens, and when the same church saw the Virgin Mary standing upon a beautiful hillside, and to our own ancestors who would not cross their knife and fork upon their plate for fear of a dire calamity, the human family has been the perfect victim of a logic which reasoned not from a basis of a universe of law, but from a basis of divine and satanic originality and caprice.

In the conscious and unconscious work of overthrowing this past, human logic was compelled to become destructive. Before, it had believed everything. Now, its first duty was to doubt. It was compelled to distrust everything in order that it might urge a reform. Luther himself was a transition between credulity and skepticism, for though he retained much superstition he plead for new light. He warred against the old church and against the old music, and against the prevailing practice of medicine, so he is seen as a point where the old is dying away and the new coming into life. Now the lesson to be inferred from these old facts is that reason has for generations near by been busy in the work of destruction. It has had to tear down a civilization badly founded and badly built, and it has, therefore, to-day, the associations of destructions, and ruins, and débris, and, at last, instead of having a habit of perfect credulity, it has reached, I fear, the habit of perfect destruction. If, as we have said, mind may form its habits, and, indeed, it evidently does form them, and if, for three hundred years, it has been destroying the awful follies of thousands of years, may we not well fear that it has come forth from this long slaughter of ideas, sighing, like an Alexander, for other worlds to conquer. When we behold a reason in thousands of public places, and in a still larger multitude in what we call "private life," busy taking down the ideas of God, and worship, and sin, and virtue, and of a future life, we cannot but feel that reason has formed, or is forming, a passion of destruction which will soon leave mankind nothing in its hands except eating, and drinking and death. As it was difficult or impossible for Alexander to combine a love of war and a love of peace, so it seems impossible for our modern reason, coming in from the glorious victories of a hundred battle-fields, to repose in the peace of the Sermon on the Mount, or the world's old cardinal truths of religion. I confess there is nothing that may command a halt to the passion of destructive criticism, for, like Napoleon, it is free to destroy worlds as long as it can find them; but while no one has power to check, yet we all have the privilege of attempting to advise or dissuade, and of commending a path better than that of destruction.

As to this destructive inquiry about God, reducing Him to an oxygen or an unconscious, unknown agency, we may well recall the fact that there is no moral proposition which may not by the same devotion to skepticism be stricken out from the catalogue of beliefs. Logic, if well followed, may lead us to doubt whether there is such a thing as beauty, whether there is such a thing as honor, such a thing as benevolence, such a thing as mind, such a thing as gratitude or pure affection. When it comes to a search for perfect assurance, then we soon ruin the moral world, for there is no perfect assurance in it or any part of it, and hence the logic which seeks that assurance can only destroy. It must come back each evening saying, "There is no virtue, no sin, no mind, no God." When logic informs you and me that God is a law or a widespread blind agency, let us not be deceived, for all it has done is to take away *our* God. It has not given us a positive origin of the universe, for if positiveness is unattainable, reason will in a few years confess itself to be as uncertain about *its* data as it is to-day about the data of the Christian. Perfect assurance is just as impossible to a *free religionist* or *atheist* as it is to the Christian. Remembering, therefore, that there is no moral idea of beauty, or love, or soul, that may not be denied, and remembering, too, that the assurance that there is a God is always logically equal to the opposite belief, why should we not abandon a criticism that only destroys, and clasp to our souls the grand things we possess, and, Christ-like, live not to destroy, but to fulfill. The worth of life, and its happiness too, have always come from the affirmation of such propositions as demand action. Life is valuable according to its love, not according to its hate. It is of little value to *hate sin* unless that implies an active love of virtue. The former gives only a refrain, a refusal to act badly, the latter gives positive virtuous action.

The "free religion," so called, which denies our

idea of prayer, dissuades from hymn, and from hope in a future life, does nothing but empty the mind and the heart, and hence can never build up a great life unless emptiness of soul is one of the foundations of greatness. All the moral greatness of the past is based upon the assumption of such notions as God and worship and immortality and benevolence, and virtue and duty. The great names all grow up out of such a soil. These propositions filled the old hearts that made this good world which we enjoy, with its education, its liberty, its morals, its religion. It is too late, it seems to me, to ask mankind to empty its mind of all these old, grand ideas, and then expect a grandeur of character to spring up from nothingness as a soil, and to grow in a space which has no rainfall, no dew, no sunshine, but which is only a vacuum. To expect a good soul to germinate in a soil of negation, and grow in a vacuum, is to cherish a frail hope, and yet this is the prospect to which what is called "free religion" is itself hastening and inviting us.

The exact antithesis of this emptying process is Jesus Christ and all who follow him. He came to fulfill. Under the method of modern unbelief the life of man daily becomes narrower. The belief in a God and the attendant worship of Him, with all its trust, and hope, and virtue, has occupied a vast space in human life; and when to this we add the kindred ideas of heaven and endless existence, we have a vast world of thought and sentiment, which, when taken away from the heart, must leave life narrow indeed. But thus exactly does the criticism of to-day narrow life and transform it from a stream that widens into an ocean into a little thread which runs between some chemical action and a grave. Modern criticism seems a pursuit of the infinitely little, a search for the microscopic atom, not only of man's body, but of his virtue and hope. Reason being just as powerful for the Christian's God as against Him, the scales should be easily turned in the Christian's favor by the weight of those positive actions, and duties, and pleasures, and hopes, with which it occupies the soul. It fills the human life to overflowing. The radical unbeliever must sit down in despair. Unbelief says, "I believe not in God, hence not in prayer, not in virtue, not in sin, not in man's greatness, not in his future beyond the grave. Hence let me alone. I shall sit here forever, and ponder and wonder, and then die." But with as much of abstract reason upon his side, the positively religious man finds no hour, no year of nothingness, but all his years, be they fourscore, are full of activity and hope. There is no eclipse of the life that now is, for it is granted every pleasure, every pursuit, ever honor, every industry. There have been religionists who have thought it necessary to make this life miserable in order that they might find joy in the next. It was the habit of semi-barbarous ages to suppose that each present thing will find its contradiction in the future, and that the poor shall be rich, and the rich poor. Following this old trace of disappointment, many not semi-barbarous still fear to be very happy to-day lest such a state will forebode evil to-morrow. For reasons evident and obscure there have been religionists, Christians indeed, who have made this life wretched that the next may be its opposite and be happy; but this folly of yesterday counts no more against Christianity than the errors of old astronomy or old politics weigh against the real truth in those sciences.

Religion grants everything to this life that belongs to human nature. It is the angel of the street and the house carrying to one integrity and benevolence, to the other love and tenderness. Did religion not come last week and wreathe your homes with evergreens and flowers, and blend with all that is joyous in youth or old age? Does it not adorn your marriage altars and breathe its benediction there, and when we bury the dead, whatever of peace and consolation there is in the last hour comes up from the lips of religion. As understood, at last, religion is the angel of joy to this world, and hence is a grand fulfilling of its most sacred longings and prophecy. And then by its vast estimate of a life beyond, by the swelling music of immortality, it expands the idea of life on this shore and thus dignifies man by loading him with this infinite outcome of himself. When Gustavus Adolphus, of Sweden, saw before him the destiny of king, his heart and mind began to live in a nobler atmosphere. In morals, in study, in heroism he immediately arose above his fellow-men and died at last leaving mankind to wonder whether he was not the noblest man that had graced earth. But this spiritual greatness he drew from the realization of a great future. Coming events cast not only their shadow, but their light and music and inspiration, before. Our positive Christianity thus not only fills each day full of its own special joy and work and peace, but it pours around the present the atmosphere of a great future, for which destiny, greater than that of a throne in Sweden, the mind and heart secretly gird themselves in their early and later years. Thus, while a destructive criticism, which in our days often passes under the name of reason, and often under the ambiguous name of "free religion," is plainly seen narrowing the life which it calls "broad," is plainly seen sitting down in despair, powerless to say more, or do more, or hope more, the positive faith of Christendom widens life in every particular of its thought or emotion or work. The religion of Christ is a wonderful fulfillment of mankind's conclusions in morals and in blessed anticipation. The great heathen world is not overthrown in the New Testament, but is fulfilled there in its essential thoughts. The morals and prayers of Aurelius and Seneca, the maxims of India, the prayers of the Greek prophets and oracles, the treasures of a past world, are found in the Gospels, as flowers cast into the fabled Alpheus were said to come forth fresh in a far-off island, at the fountain of Arethusa. A distinguished teacher recently from Siam says that the Buddhists accept of Christ most readily when they compare his spiritual teachings with their own, and thus find him to be only the perfection of their own reason and sentiment. They love him when they find that he has not come to destroy, but only to lead higher by a similar but more sublime flight.

The lessons, therefore, which I would offer to those here this morning who may not be members of any Christian church, and who after this closing service may not perhaps, all of them at least, depend upon this place and hour for any Sunday morning lesson in religion, are these:

(1) In a critical age that has so many errors to be destroyed, reason acquires a destructive habit; and against this habit one must guard, lest instead of being a light to guide us, reason becomes only a mildew to blight a world once beautiful.

(2) The soul grows great and useful and happy, not by what it denies, but by what it cordially affirms and loves. Distrust is the death of the soul, belief is its life. The just shall live by faith. Infidelity is the abandonment of life — a suicide of the spirit.

(3) Should you not all seek union with some positive, active, singing, praying, trusting church? What errors any Christian church may hold will not harm half so much as its active truths will bless. Let the church you seek be "free," not free in its unbelief, free in its atheism, but free in its deliverance from superstition, and free in its noble manhood, that fears no one but God. Let the church you seek be *broad*, but not broad in its destructiveness, but in its soul and hopes and charity; not broad by the absence of God, but by His infinite presence; not broad like the Sahara in its treeless, birdless, dewless sands; not broad like the Arctic sea in perpetual silence and ice,

but broad like an infinite paradise, full of all verdure, all fruits, all music, all industry, all happiness, all worship, wide enough in its gates and confines to repeat the Savior's invitation, "Come," to all the children of this outer wilderness.

CHRISTIANITY AS A CIVILIZATION.

SERMON XI.

CHRISTIANITY AS A CIVILIZATION.

"And he shall sit as a refiner and purifier of silver."—*Mal. 3 : 3.*

IN discussing the proposition suggested by this text, that Christianity is a civilization, it will be necessary to think of civilization in two lights—the one as the condition of the individual, the other as a power to influence others standing apart from its condition. What mankind needs is not simply a picture of an elevated human life, but also an agency that will rapidly cast men into the likeness of this ideal picture. Individuals have always been visible here and there who have, in their minds and hearts, reflected the features of almost the ideal manhood, but their virtues have been unable to multiply themselves infinitely in the outer world; and living, they never perceived virtue to have gone out from their garments at a world's touch; and dying, they have taken their moral excellence into their tombs, as Beatrice took away her beauty with her, and as the dying songstress recently took with her, forever, her warm melody. History is dotted over with names of such piety as marked Aurelius, and Cato, and Xenophon; but as between the stars of heaven, there are awful solitudes across which light itself flies invisible, and which no sound of even thunder or softest music has ever blessed, so between these isolated characters of the past, there have lived and died countless millions of the human family, without excellence and without hope — awful solitudes of the soul. In seeking, therefore, for a desirable civilization, it is necessary for us to find a culture that will overflow. We seek a Nile that shall cross its banks in June, and make the whole adjoining empire pass from a wilderness to a garden. That this is what we should seek may be learned in an instant by a glance at the world, for that glance reveals the fact that the moral harvest of any one age is only a reduplication of the seed sown in the age before; that, for example, the Christian church is only a reduplication of the Seventy, the Seventy a harvest from the Twelve, the Twelve an overflow from Christ, with Christ himself an outreaching from eternity. Thus it becomes perfectly evident that when we seek a civilization, we must find one, if possible, that possesses the aggressive power and genius that will open out, fan-like, and pass from one to many, incapable of rest as to labor, and as to its aspirations and conquests. Christianity seems to me to surpass all other reforms in these two needed particulars; it presents us with a high type of manhood, and a manhood that flows outward from one to many. Let us, then, direct our attention first to the Christian character as a civilization.

Impossible or difficult as it may be to find a definition of civilization, it will answer the demands of the hour in which we meet together as a public, common assemblage, and not as exact philosophers, if we state that man is civilized when all his faculties of mind and heart are active within their spheres, not falling short of Nature's law nor going beyond it. Under "faculties" must be included conscience and all the tender sentiments of friendship, love, sympathy, and religion, for without these a character may possess greatness in many respects, but not that perfect blending which seems to give us the perfect manhood. The word whose definition we seek primarily means fitted for organized society, fitted for the state. The wild man, whose club is his law, may become so transformed in thousands of years that he is fitted, at last, for a home in a community, where many ages and conditions and qualities of soul meet with equal rights, and where egotism must give place to the confession of others. Out of the peculiar demands of society, demands for reciprocity, for kindness, for liberality of thought, for respect to law and morals, and out of the mental and æsthetic culture which the wise state brings, to be fitted for state life soon came to be synonymous with the idea of perfect manhood. Edmund Burke says: "The spirit of civilization is composed of two parts, the spirit of a gentleman and the spirit of religion." This is only another way of informing us that civilization is a life lived as in the presence of man and God. But cull the definition from what fields you may, and express it in what words you prefer, and yet the New Testament, through Christ in His discourses, or through Paul in his letters, will surpass all other analyses, from sources modern or ancient. When to personal purity of deed, and even of thought, Christ adds the command to love one's neighbor as one's self and to be kind even to enemies, he has reached the ideal; for when the wave of virtue flows within the heart, and the wave of good deeds flows outside, all around, we have found a manhood full armed for life in its varied responsibilities. It would seem that Paul, in his chapter upon charity, was expressly describing the perfect gentleman. "Charity suffereth long and is kind. Charity envieth not. Charity boasteth not itself, is not puffed up, doth not behave itself unseemly, seeketh not her own, is not easily provoked, thinketh no evil, rejoiceth not in iniquity, but rejoiceth in the truth; beareth all things, believeth all things, hopeth all things, endureth all things." Evidently in living up to such a picture we should all make a grand approach toward a civilized life. It was truly said by the free-thinking Mrs. Jameson that "Christianity is a beautiful civilization." From causes which we cannot enumerate here, publicists have been unwilling to look at the religion of the Bible in any other light than that of a special mode of escape from future ills, ills beyond the grave; and wishing to study the philosophy of states, the conditions of a good citizenship here, have turned over all heathen pages and over all other pages not set apart by and for a priesthood. It has long been a custom of philosophic minds to pass in silence any lessons of civilization upon the pages of Scripture, and patiently to seek and deeply to love everything in Aristotle or Plato—a blossoming of prejudice only paralleled by the Christians who despise everything from Plato or Aristotle.

Permit me now to assume that the truly Christian character is a highly civilized character, for this is not an important branch of our inquiry. To discover a good analysis of the ideal man is not so difficult as it is to find some power that may induce the largest number to come up toward this ideal.

Hence, our second proposition, that Christianity possesses in a large measure the power to influence those standing afar off, is the question of most interest and the work of most difficulty, for even could we draw from the classic or Hindoo world a complete definition of manhood we should seem to need a Christ to enable the human race to realize the dream betrayed in the definition.

In order to produce a universal manhood, we must find a truth that overflows, a philosophy the opposite of *egoism*, a philosophy deeply altruistic. Our world of love must include our neighbor—for human welfare does not spring only from what one has, but from what this favored one *can or will give away.* A religion in which one good man becomes ten good men is the only one that will offer society hope. Now the grand attribute of Christ and His method is this living for others. Christ Himself was a putting aside of Heaven's peace and joy for earth's sorrow, a springing away from His own life and a descent into human life. His heart burst the limitations of self, and so loved the world that He scattered, as it were, the garments of His own glory over the unclothed human race, that they might each possess a wedding garment, and He opened over earth an urn of righteousness that sinners, poor in such riches, might gather up this manna, rained down in the night, and be just at last before God. Thus, if there is one sentence which more than others may express the genius of this Christ, it is this: "He was a goodness that rolled outward, a love whose rays, like those of the sun, darted away from itself. How far the light of our sun may fly before it becomes invisible! Let us suppose an earth ten times as far away as our own, would still catch some daily smiles from that orb, you can imagine what a vast circle, two thousand millions of miles wide, would all be filled perpetually by the light of that central fire. In the world of morals, Christianity is a love which thus from one heart moves outward and contemplates nothing less than shining upon each face that is seen or shall be seen walking the paths in this vale. Christianity is not by accident nor by common natural law only, but by its whole special genius and yearnings, a contagion of truth and virtue. As God placed in the grain of wheat a hidden germ by which that one grain will become a hundred, and will not by any means remain in its *egoism* unless it die, so in the religion of Jesus there is an implanted longing, such that no Christ-like soul will consent to walk along through life or to heaven without wishing to drag all society with it to the sublime destiny. It would be vain, so far as all society is thought of, if Christ's religion held only good doctrines for individual hearts, for only here and there one would find them, just as Marcus Aurelius found piety and Zenobia virtue. It is not enough that faith in the Divine Being is a saving influence, and that repentance is also a saving grace, and that a new heart is possible, and that pardon is possible in the Christian system; but, given these great paths to heaven, it is essential that those who find them receive along with them a desire to hurl their sunlight outward upon faces standing in the valley and shadow of death. Above all other systems Christianity is an aggressive civilization. Its hearts are in Greenland to-day among the snows, and in Ceylon among the flowers, in Africa among the negroes, in Oregon among the Indians, bearing all hardships, because their religion is the overthrow of self and the enthronement of mankind; an imitation of the cross where the blessedness of the multitude was purchased by the sorrows of one.

Having seen now that Christianity possesses the two elements of a civilization, the ideal and the power to spread the ideal, let us defend it against some parts of its history. Our age alone is the fortunate one that has come anywhere near reading aright the religion of Christ. I will confess that all intermediate ages have attempted to spread their religion, but almost the only element they drew from their Divine Savior was the desire to make their faith universal. But what the faith was, or how to make their neighbor receive it, they seem never to have dreamed. It does not argue against a sentiment that men have erred as to what path it should follow. The Hindoo mother loves her child and often for that reason tosses it to the Ganges god; and there was an old nation once in which filial love made it customary to put the old father and mother to death when their powers were well along in decline; and yet the sentiments of maternal and filial love are sacred sentiments, and ask only that they may flow in the channels of pure reason. Thus the zeal for spreading religion is Christ-like, and is the hope of the world, but it must make no mistake and slaughter a group of Jews or burn an infidel, for in doing so it sustains the same relation to a religious sentiment that the mother sustains to the maternal instinct who offers her child to a god, or that the children sustain to filial love who put to death their grand, old, loving parents. When we read in the reign of Frederick that when a Christian child disappeared it was customary to rush forth and accuse and kill a few Jews, and that three hundred Jews were put to death on account of the disappearance of three boys, which boys were afterward found in a stream, where they had been, all alone, playing upon the ice, and had broken in without any Jewish assistance, we can no more reproach Christianity than we may charge religion in general with the deaths under juggernaut, or with the burning of widows. In all that cruel era there was little trace of Christ as unfolded in the Testament; and in a large part of the era when church and state were identified little remained of Christianity except the disposition to spread itself; it lost all else; it defined itself to be *power* and spread itself by the sword. While, however, with the calmest minds the actual history of this sublime religion does not vitiate its theory, yet, it being a fact that the great public is not remarkable for calm justice, confidence in Christianity as a reform seems to-day greatly shaken, and it will need all the wisdom and piety and tenderness of its friends for a century to make it stand forth before the human race as the most complete savior of men. I fully believe that this religion of Jesus could be so preached, and so lived, and so applied to society, that in two generations a pure rationalism (excluding the supernatural) or a cold materialism would nowhere be taught; and that legislators and statesmen would begin their careers by a study of Christ as a teacher and an impulse. Suppose that in all the next half century the church should resume the idea of an *overflowing* religion, as Christ held it and acted it; that, widening out from fashionable avenues and costly churches, and the luxury of a saint's rest, it should reach out its hands to the poor and build a score of neat churches in this city, furnished with organ and books, and with a teacher for each who understood and loved the populace; imagine the whole church to change its whole policy for this fifty years, and, instead of running from the multitudes, actually turn and go toward them, as the women are now going toward the crowds, carrying, not an abstract definition of Trinity and atonement, but prayers and hymns, and a sufficient, inviting, persuading, mediating Christ, and if Christianity did not in the end wring from the world the confession that it alone is a civilizing power worthy of earth and heaven, then it would seem that the relation between cause and effect is only a delusion. Open this religion and you will see the wheels of a great machine. As the ponderous engine hurls the steamship from America to England, makes it run like a vast shuttle from shore to shore, thus the gospel of Christ lies ready to move all society, and make it fly from vice to virtue, though wide is the dark sea between. But not yet has the church put this machinery into motion. When our government, a few years ago, gave the Japanese a locomotive and car, and put down for them a circle of track, that foreign land was delighted; but, strange delight! it led the officials to go upon festal days and ride around the magic iron ring, giving them a schoolboy happiness, but not leading them to throw a line quickly across the empire. Are you prepared to deny that thus we have used the Christian religion? Have we not kept it for home use and refused to fling it across the empire? Instead of preaching the gospel to ten thousand people is not each clergyman employed to preach it ten thousand times to the same people? The life of Christ, the life of His disciples, the history of all revivals from Paul's day to Wesley's and Whitefield's and to our own Moody's, announce the genius of Christianity to be that of *outgoing* love, a love which grows by going and dies in any confinement, in any repose.

This trait of ideal Christianity that is an action rather than a philosophy has been often the accidental cause of its shame, as well as the perpetual cause of its honor. A prominent reason why the reforms of Mill and Comte and *The Westminster Review* have remained so beautiful is to be found in the fact that they have descended into the dust of actual work. It is not Comte or Tyndall who must plead with the begrimed miners of England, it is Moody and Sankey. Hence upon these last names must gather all the associations of the ragged clothes, the superstition and fanaticism of the crowd. From Gibbon to Huxley, rationalism has never stirred up the untaught multitude, but has enjoyed the better association of porches of philosophy and shelves of walnut in the library. When we saw in the exposition the many elegantly painted reaping machines, we stole a glance into the future and pictured them as they would appear after they had been dragged over the prairies from June to September. The rational methods have received greetings in the temples of learning and art, and we behold the whiteness of their vesture and their calmness of face, and on the other side we behold the Christian Idea with the forehead marked with care and browned in the sun, but we forgive this marred beauty, for we know in what wide fields of time and eternity she has toiled since Bethlehem, and upon us bursts the vision of *One* "whose visage was so marred more than any man, and His form more than the sons of men." So far as rationalistic reforms have escaped the historic association of fanaticism and bloody persecutions, so far as they have burned no Servetus and banished no Quakers, the desirable result must be attributed in part to the fact that they are a theory more than a life; the opposite of Christianity, for the moment it learns of its Master and its heaven, it rushes forth and permits the beggar to associate his rags with this Jesus, and the Methodist to pierce his sky with shouts, the temperance women to kneel in the streets, and the African slaves to sing rude hymns all night long in a strange ecstacy around this cross.

Christ has stood so near the people that they have wreathed his cross with their infirmities at the very hour when they crowded around it to find their salvation. And it is this nearness to the human heart which has made Christianity drench with blood fields over which infidelity would have whispered "peace," for religion has always been an active, powerful sentiment, and hence its errors have been as active as its truths. As jealousy attends love and is impossible in cold, indifferent hearts, so often cruelty has gathered about religion in its dark cloud; but those awful facts reveal a passion which shall become the world's hope far beyond any promise which a cold, intellectual reform can ever offer to mankind. As love in a wrong path, or itself wronged, may become an agony and a cruelty, but in its full light and wisdom opens out into a paradise, so Christianity, escaping from errors of doctrine and practice, opening forth in all its fullness of truth and in all its divineness of method — a method by which one heart transfers its truth and hope to its neighbor's heart — flowing beyond old channels and breaking over into the fields of the poor, poor in gold and in virtue; thus rushing outward with Christ everywhere for its leader and motive, Christianity, I repeat, will either become the world's civilization or else we must bow in sorrow and declare the generations to come of sin and wrong, to be utterly without hope. It may not be easy to feel that Christ's gospel shall reform the world, for the world is so vast that our feeble minds may be forgiven if they are appalled at the task, but it seems easy to feel that this gospel is the only hope, for to truths the most divine and the most complete, omitting nothing that pertains to mind, body, and soul, that pertains to the now or the future, it goes beyond this rare excellence and adds that without which all truth is vain, a spiritual awakening and inspiration. It is not ideas alone that transform the world, but ideas with an inspiration in them crowding them from dream to life. The truths of Christ's reform possess that impulse which comes from their lying out-spread not only in the light of earth, but in that of eternity. Not only the happiness of society here is in them, but hell and heaven fill them up with their awful or sweet mystery, their fear and hope. But their cup of virtues is not yet full, for Christ is in it also not as a teacher only, who is simply remembered, but as an ever-present spirit cheering the soul to-day just as he blessed men eighteen hundred years ago; and if the heart need anything more it may find it in the consciousness that the Father of all, the Almighty, lies under these ideal truths, lifting them up into life as He moves the ocean into storm or smiles.

Here, then, is a reform adequate in its truths and in its motives. What detains it from its great mission? It waits simply for man. It waits for the church to escape from the letter which killeth to the spirit which giveth life; it waits for the Christian throng to enter, not their sanctuary only, vocal with music and eloquence, but the world, vocal with wailings and eloquent with tears; waits for its ministry to pass from doctrines which confuse the intellect and transform the church into a school of debate, to the doctrines which lie upon human life like a child upon its mother's heart, dear and inseparable; waits for a breadth of mind and soul to come that will not contract theology into the limits of a stagnant pool, but will expand it into an ocean such that along with faith and repentance all the charities, and all liberty, and all culture, and all the great temperance pleadings, shall seem also cardinal doctrines of God, weaving the wreath of His glory, and issuing from His throne to man in garments more radiant for earth than any, which, far away from human sense, flow around the profound mysteries of religion.

ST. PAUL.

SERMON XII.

ST. PAUL.

THE immense amount of attention given, within recent years, to the relation of Paul to Christianity, warrants us in drawing some inferences regarding that prominent character, at least justifies us in making him a theme of brief remark. It will be years yet before the position of St. Paul can be fully defined, and for this closing up of accounts none of us can afford to wait. It is the privilege of each year to gather up the approximations of truth that appear within its own bounds, and, pending the final decision, to derive what cheer or help it may from the evidence rendered up to the passing hour. As in the trial of some great personage the public does not await in solemn silence the closing of the case and the decision of the court, but irresistibly follows each witness and weighs the testimony each hour, so, in the progress of moral inquiry, one cannot sit down and wait for the end, but, by the mind's nature, is led along through a series of weights and measurements in succeeding days. There is no provision made in the mind for perfect repose. It is commanded us by nature to go on. Like the Wandering Jew, in the fable, we must march, march, march!

But the following obligation should be confessed, namely, that the newer the inquiry, the greater the number of facts not yet brought in, the greater should be the modesty and charity of the wondering crowd, hoping, longing, fearing, as they stand around the witnesses and the box of the accused. Before the vast inquiries now opening up like a river that approaches the sea — inquiries rising under the name of Darwin or Huxley, one need not sit down in silence, but may only proceed with the charity and humility of children diffident in their helpless youth. If all inferences must cease until inquiries are wholly ended, life is reduced to a sleep that needs waking only once in a hundred years.

In all the present inquiry about St. Paul, there is no vital idea involved. Hence, nothing is to be feared, even if not much were to be hoped. How far he differed from the other apostles, how far he was designed of God to give shape and tone to the church, how far he has done so, what were his views, what his genius, how far his teachings were local, how far universal — are inquiries that involve no calamity, and hence need produce no passion, no trembling among Christians, nor boastings among infidel hearts. The inquiry promises good to the church far more than it forebodes any evil. Paul seems a power only half-weighed, half-prized in the past. The new attention of the present seems to be the return of the Christian mind to a better estimate of its own outfit and resources.

An age afar off may better read a man or a system than an age that was near, because it may bring to the task a more congenial mind and heart. That the church has reached a point eighteen centuries away from St. Paul is no proof that it ever exhausted, or even fully studied, the details of the doctrine, or spirit of the apostle. It often happens that a thousand years come between an event and any careful study of the event. Men are diverted by some new issue, and then by some other issue, and for hundreds of years make no sign of return to any objects that stood by their starting point. Thus Aristotle unfolded the inductive philosophy; but men turned away from it, and never came near it again until in the far-off days of Lord Bacon. Astronomy flourished in old Egypt, and was quite complete and truthful; but the public mind deserted it, and returned not until in modern periods. Thus men are always making long and great wanderings, and great and beautiful returns.

In Mexico and South America, there are old mines of silver and gold, where, hundreds of years ago, shafts were sunk and furnaces were busy separating the metal from dust. But upspringing war, or decay of industry, or growth of vice, drew away the toilers, and left the mines to the silence of those many years. Now, the new status assumed by the nineteenth century sends men back to the mines, and new shafts are sunk, and new furnaces blaze in the long-deserted valleys of the precious ores. In religion, the ages desert rich veins, and, after decay has hung for centuries about the old shafts, back come their remote children, and, with double energy and intelligence, make the gold and silver distil from the old earth. They return with better science, and secure a richer yield.

The early tendency of the church toward temporal power, drew away from the spirituality of Christ and from the broad republicanism of St. Paul. The fact that Peter was represented as having the keys, and being the rock upon which the church was founded, drew the attention of the early half-barbarous church toward that one apostle, and for fifteen hundred years Peter was the ideal genius of the Christian establishment. Not the absolute Peter of the Testament, but the idealized Peter of Romanism —Peter with human embellishment, Peter transformed into a colossus. One can perceive this transformation and enthronement of this apostle, not only in the fact that he was made pope and was followed by a regular succession, but even in the sculpture and painting of the middle ages in which arts Peter always enjoyed the richest colors and robes, and the whitest blocks of marble. Moses, David, Peter, were the favorites of the artists.

Innocently, and even unconsciously, St. Paul was left under a cloud. He was so world-wide, so separated from forms and from localities, that, to the half-civilized ages he was almost invisible, while Peter with keys in his hand and with the suspicion of being a rock upon which a church could be built for the keys to lock and unlock, became very visible indeed. That which men wish to see is always the most visible. With the ideas that Paul held, that forms were of little value, that neither circumcision nor uncircumcision availed, that neither meat or no meat, holy days or no holy days, contained any merit, that nothing was of any value except the new creature, the new soul within, it was impossible for him to rise into first notice and first love in an age to which forms had been the dearest and best thing. The world was oligarchic, despotic, aristocratic, in all its education and hopes. Empire was its largest idea. Peter, supposed to be a rock of government, and supposed to possess keys, was, therefore, worth a thousand times more than St. Paul, who was an exponent of man universal, and of a religion of only the heart. Peter stood for empire, Paul for the soul.

Such an age did not, and would not, calmly weigh the two ideas, the Paul and Peter, and declare Peter to suit and delight it the more. It would simply grasp Peter by its instinct. It would not deliberately reject Paul. It would never dream of his being anything valuable. When Indians select colored beads and ribbons from white explorers, they do not condemn the books, the laws, the schools of the white race. They do nothing and think nothing on the subject. They grasp by instinct, and lay hold upon gaudy colors and objects of sense. So the early church did not rationally condemn Paul; it reached out its arms by instinct and grasped the man that possessed the keys of power. The act was that of a child, not that of a philosopher. Accustomed to an empire, it grasped for a sword as did the infant Achilles.

In this unconscious neglect, Christ Himself suffered, not a little, along with his apostle. It was, of course, impossible for any age wholly to overlook Christ. Paul was one of twelve, and could be escaped; but Christ was one of one. He was alone. But what was denied the age in the power to ignore, it atoned for in the power to interpret badly. Compelled to see Christ, it interpreted Him by its own instinct, and made of Him a regal prince anxious to grind to powder many enemies, and to exalt a few friends. The monarchic instinct that doomed Paul to obscurity, doomed the Christ to the similitude of a rude King, rather than clothed Him with the beauty of a Savior. And thus the great cloud, composed of keys of empire, of material things, of forms, of thrones, of princes and slaves, of pomp and circumstance, threw its shadow far down the valley of human life, even down to the Pilgrims and Puritans.

Paul and his Master, belonging to a new era, to one of spirituality and human equality, it was necessary for them both to lie in partial shadow until their new era should come. If there was an instinct that could grasp the literal keys and local empire, so there would be an instinct that would grasp a new life and a kingdom of man universal. Paul, along with his Savior, must wait for this. Fitted for a spiritual life, they must stand still until the pageant of Peter had passed by.

Another great shadow followed the church. It was that of the Mosaic age. Moses and David were grand monarchs. Their brilliant power and severe institutions have haunted the Christian era in all its long career. Notwithstanding the sermons of Christ, and the terrible eloquence of St. Paul about the dissolution of the Mosaic economy, the empire of the Hebrew state was so deeply in harmony with the taste of bishops and popes, that the laws of Moses carried away the study and love that belonged to the Sermon on the Mount, and the new truths of the Pauline letters. The Mosaic age died slowly. As by long paths ages come, by long paths they depart. This shadow of Hebrew power followed the church, not only up to the reformation of Luther, but up to the Pilgrim Fathers, who still wished to seize upon some country as Moses had seized upon Palestine, and to banish Quakers and Huguenots, as Moses had silenced the Philistines and Amorites.

The fact that the Westminster Assembly passed its laws as to what is required and what forbidden in the Ten Commandments, and neglected to inquire what is enjoined and what forbidden in the Sermon on the Mount, shows that the empire of Moses was still intruding itself upon the presence of Christ. It is not to be wondered at that in all these long centuries the more spiritual and liberal ideas of St. Paul lay in the oblivion of neglect. Full of universal love, reckless of geographical lines, hostile to the outward, devoted to the new life, wholly separate from earthly power and kings, living beyond Moses as manhood outranks infancy, and rapt in the vision of Jesus Christ, Paul was compelled to wait until the rise of liberty should destroy alike the scepter of Moses and the scepter of the pope. He waited the time to lead mankind to a religion of the spirit, and to the Sermon on the mountain side.

Luther unveiled the image of Paul. That hand lifted some of the heaviest drapery. A thousand material things were consumed by his touch, and the faith of the soul in Jesus Christ became brilliantly visible. Luther thundered against penance and works just as Paul thundered against the outward forms of the Jews; and against popes and states just as Paul had declaimed against an earthly Jerusalem and the caste of the Hebrews. Luther was one of the first flowers of the seed sown by the Saint. Then followed the wide German and English efflorescence. In such mortals as John Wesley and Whitefield and Duff, and almost the whole school of those men, the soul of Paul beams forth — a sun that had been long clouded. They are all the abandonment of the papal idea, and are the escape from the shadow of the Mosaic age. They are a reproduction of Christ; an acceptance of the church of Jesus and Paul.

Paul's ideas, those of democracy, of spirituality, instead of ceremony, of attachment to Jesus Christ, were too great for the first fifteen centuries. They must needs lead a semi-life until the spread of intelligence and republicanism should help abolish rites, and place all men upon one level, not only before God, but, what is more difficult, before men. An age will never accept anything at discord with itself. An aristocratic State will demand aristocratic religion, schools and amusements. An ignorant, superstitious country will require a superstitious literature and religion. The stories they tell their children will be about ghosts and wonders. As an iron magnet will gather up nothing but the dust of itself, will lift nothing but kindred iron, so an age will lay hold of no idea out of harmony with its heart. Monarchy grasped Moses and St. Peter, and let fall all else. Universal liberty reaches out for its own children and draws to its bosom Christ and his large-souled apostle. The development that has plucked iron crowns from the foreheads of kings has plucked them from the foreheads of priests, and has given us not only a people's government, but a people's Savior.

But for Paul, it is thought by many students of history that Judaism would have carried its circumcision and seclusiveness and awful despotism right forward for perhaps a thousand years. It would have wound the thorns of the State laws around the body of Christ, a wreath of pain and despair around a symbol of hope. The revolt of St. Paul weakened the old dispensation, and led John and the subsequent Christians into the beginnings of a new career. Paul's steady light abates the Mosaic shadow.

All history, profane and sacred, contains proofs that God embodies His truth in some human heart, buries it there and commands it to blossom as fast as men give it sunshine enough, and only so fast. In the bosom of Moses there lay ideas beyond his people. They laughed them and him to scorn. But in a few centuries the Hebrew commonwealth grew grand all over with the outgrowth of Mosaic truths. Not grand compared with a modern ideal, but compared with what was and had been. In the outset Moses was too great for his people. In the end the people had caught up with their leader. No phenomenon is more frequent. In St. Paul was buried the gospel of spirituality, of humanity, of a pure heart, and of Jesus Christ.

The first idea of spirituality sounded the death knell of forms. Circumcision or uncircumcision would avail naught, but the "new creature."

The second idea, "all humanity," abolished popes

and powers, fagots and proscription, the exaltation of the creed of Apollos or Cephas, and raised a slave to the rank of a son of God.

The third idea of a pure life announced the end of salvation by means of a complex machinery of doctrine and the dawn of a new era of honesty and piety.

The fourth idea, Jesus Christ, yesterday, to-day and forever, cast Christianity into the form of a personal friendship and love for the Divine Savior. For Paul to live was Christ, — to die, gain, because death sent him to Christ. The world resolved itself into the presence of the Savior.

In Paul's bosom, more than in any other human heart, were planted these ideas — four rivers in the paradise of religion. As when Moses came down from the mount his face was radiant with a light not visible to those around him, but streaming off to beat upon shores five hundred years away, as Galileo and Bacon spoke words that were unheard by those nearest, but were borne by some strange reverberation to a multitude afar off, so Paul, more divinely, carried in his bosom truth-germs destined to blossom far away from the tomb of his dust. Perhaps these seeds are now disturbing the soil of this century.

Think of these great ideas. Spirituality! This is nothing else than a divineness of soul, a rising above things material, gold and lands and raiment, and living for the soul in its relations to time and eternity. God is called a spirit because there are characteristics in all material things which separate them from perfection. The word spirit is the ideal for the everlasting. It is an embodiment of love, and of thought, and of truth, and of life, and hence is felt to be immortal. The spiritual man is hence a soul not wedded to dust, but to truth, love and life. To be spiritually minded is life. In Paul's grand religion rites availed nothing. Circumcision, baptism, set days, sects of Paul and Apollos, were all of no moment compared with that spiritual cast of the soul, able, like angels' wings, to bear man to immortality.

Look at his second idea. The oneness of humanity! Oh sublime sentiment! Had Catharine de Medici known it, she would have clasped the Huguenots to her bosom and said, "I love you all." Had Calvin felt its infinite tenderness, he would have thrown his arms about Servetus and said, "Live and be happy, my brother. I differ with you, but love you." But this idea must await the birth of democracy.

Look at Paul's third idea. A new life, a new creature! It will be the development of this idea that will announce the dawn of a perfect civilization and a golden age.

The church has tried the religion of dogmas. The Scotch churches reached a creed of thousands of articles, but that church, and all branches of all churches, have furnished thousands of men for every branch of dishonesty and crime.

The men that commit acts of crime and dishonor, the men who commit frauds in the money circles, come, in part, from the multitude that carry a Catechism or a Book of Common Prayer. All this because religion has been a form of argument rather than a shape of the inner life. Oh blessed age will that be when a holy life shall be the aim and significance of religion, and when it shall be universally confessed that unless one has the spirit of Christ he is none of His.

But, passing all these, look at Paul's fourth passion. Love for Jesus Christ! I shall say little here because the measurement of words fail.

In sounding the sea, places were found where the lead failed; and for hours the vessel would sail with the sounding line coiled on its bow, there being no use for it in the awful silence beneath. Paul's attachment to Jesus Christ is beyond our cold, feeble measurement. For him to live was Christ. To die was gain, for the soul joined its Friend. As children live for the happiness that spring and summer and winter promise to their glad hearts; as they long for the morning because of the new pleasure it will bring; as for them to live is pleasure; as Pitt and Burke and Webster lived for country, and honor, and human law; as for them to live was fame and greatness, so for Paul to live was Jesus Christ. He slept and awoke in that sacred prepossession. To die would be gain, because the great golden cloud that enveloped him did not belong to earth, but was only the outskirt of a radiance that threw its sheen forward from the vast sea of endless life.

My dear friends, measure these four ideas of Paul, and behold in them the coming glory of Christianity and the coming blessedness of man. Liberty and intelligence are the conditions of society that are able to accept of these four ideas of religion. And as liberty and intelligence are gradually advancing, so these essentials of Christianity are rising more and more upon the soul's horizon. Science cannot injure them. The welfare of society will make men always return to them. They will always prove too useful to be destroyed, too truthful to be denied, too comforting in life and in death to remain unloved.

FAITH.

SERMON XIII.

FAITH.

"He that believeth on the Son hath everlasting life, but he that believeth not the Son shall not see life, but the wrath of God abideth on him."—*John 3:36.*

THE proposition that the soul is saved by faith in Christ involves the two inquiries, (1) What is salvation? and (2) What is faith?

Salvation must, in its final definition, be the rescue of the soul from that which is to that soul, or has been, or will be, a ruin. If there is a moral condition that may be designated by the word *lost*, then salvation is the escape of the soul from that condition. If ignorance is a loss—a ruin—then education is a salvation in that field; if poverty is a lost estate, then riches are a salvation; if mental weakness were a lost empire, the salvation would be found in a new genius, a new culture. By such illustration we may perceive that where moral depravity makes up the idea of *lost soul*, moral excellence will contain what is meant by salvation. Salvation of man, therefore, must be man's transformation from a sinful to a holy nature. It is a return of that which was lost. A legal salvation may be a preliminary or a concomitant, but cannot, in morals, be the chief salvation. In the financial department of life a debtor can be saved by having his debts paid. Condemned to death, a criminal can be saved by a letter of pardon having upon it the seal of a king; but in morals, a salvation is not simply a discharge from a debt, or an escape from a penalty, but a change in the spirit, a transition from vice to virtue. The term, therefore, draws its deepest interpretation from the term *lost*. If man is *lost* in wickedness, he is *found* again in a perfection of moral character. If my calamity is hunger, food is my release; if my soul's calamity is sin, virtue is my only rescue. In law there is such a thing as technical danger or technical safety. In the dark Kansas days there was such a thing as "constructive treason," a treason inferred from resemblance to real treason; but there can be no such thing as an inferential salvation, a constructive release, a technical escape. The meaning of the term is to be determined by its location. In morals salvation is spiritual perfection. The forgiveness of past sins, the payment of a moral debt may be preliminaries, or attendant events, and may, by their importance, aspire to the name of a rescue; but these titles are the gift of gratitude rather than of fact, for after a man's sins are all forgiven or atoned for, he stands forth still *lost*, for he retains the low nature that produces sins and made necessary the pardon or the atonement. If to us, lost in a wilderness, without a sun, or a star, or a path to guide, there comes a benevolent hermit, a dear mentor, and leads us to the right path, and sets our faces homeward, he is at once our savior; but our perfect salvation will come from our *going that path.* Our *going* and the *mentor* combine in the escape; and yet he lives in memory as the kind savior of our bewildered hearts.

Pardon and atonement form parts of the great salvation, but the vast idea is only fully met and satisfied by the word righteousness. If a departure from righteousness was man's fall, a return to it will be his safety, the heaven of the soul. If this be true, then Christ is a Savior in so far as He helps man back to that high place from which he fell in this career. The cross is only an essential prelude to the new life. The sigh of the suffering life and death of Jesus was only the solemn introduction to a great melody, in whose music should be combined the many strings of a new soul and a new career. All of sin was then finished, all of holiness was then begun. To all Christians the cross should not be the only emblem of religion, but over it should be flung, or around it wreathed the white robe of virtue, to buy which the cross was reared, and the life lived, and the death died. If salvation began at a cross, it ended not there. Its great result is reached only in the word holiness, for if in the image of God man was made, to that image Christ leads man back.

Moral perfection being the final import of the word salvation, the faith that saves the soul will need to appear on the arena as a power that will cast its possessor forward toward this perfection. If by sin man fell, it will be necessary for a saving doctrine in order to merit such a name, that it shall possess some power to lead the heart back to virtue, and it should do this by some natural law, because a perpetual miracle may not be expected unless a constant force acting naturally is impossible. If the Creator works his will elsewhere by means of regular orders of sequence, and makes the rain and sun and soil throw upward all the grand flora of earth, if He makes the great central sun the fountain of heat and motion, so that all activity falls down from it in the great flood of light, so in the domain of religion it may well be expected that God will establish some faculty of the soul that will always push upward its moral leaves and bloom, or cherish it in its life-giving warmth. Religion impresses belief into its service, because belief is a permanent law of intellectual life. Faith is this perpetual natural force. It is not an arbitrary basis of salvation any more than sunlight and rain are an arbitrary basis of flowers. Faith in Christ is a rich soil of which righteousness is the gorgeous bloom. Faith is not imposed upon the human family, as a condition of heaven, simply by the decree of God passed for Christianity alone, a despotic shibboleth separating souls differing only in the ability or non-ability to pronounce consonants, but it enters the gospel through the gate of reason or universal law written by the Creator; a law that belief shall be the basis of all religious or secular life. The doctrines that must enter into the soul's welfare are based upon the reason of God, and hence are explicable by the reason of man. In the pulpit's fear of rationalism it has often made sad havoc of its supposed outfit of common sense.

Faith is the drift of one's heart and mind in morals. All definitions of it as being a belief in things not well known, or a belief in testimony, or in doctrines hard to understand, are wasted words, for children, to whom no doctrine is difficult, and with whom all is perfectly *well known* and with whom distinctions are impossible, have an unbounded faith in God and in Christ. Faith is evidently the soul's attachment to a being. The New Testament is as wont to say "lovest thou me" as "believest thou" me. It sums up all the commandments by the word "love," and neglects the word "faith" for many a page. The followers of Christ so loved him, so gathered about his feet, Magdalen-like, bathing them with tears, that under the word "faith" we see flying along a spiritual sentiment, an angel of admiration and devotion. Faith, then, is the moral drift of the heart. It is an inner genius, ever growing, ever self-developing. It is an impulse of the soul, combining the two elements of a firm belief and a deep attachment. It is therefore both an intellectual act and a sentiment; for as when you look out upon the sea, earth or sky, in admiration of the manifold grandeur unveiled, the eye and ear and intellect are busy gathering up the scene, making sudden measurements of height or depth, sudden perception of color and sound, and after this rapid ingathering comes the sentiment of the beautiful, a deep joy, a great tone of heavenly music in the heart; thus Christian faith is both a perception and a sentiment, for gathering up the phenomena of Christ's life and death, reaching out toward his cross and purity and paradise and eternal life, it becomes a great intellect grasping a spiritual landscape, and then in the feelings that follow, of joy, forgiveness, hope, repose, it becomes a sentiment pervading the soul. It thus becomes the rational foundation of a new life. When the English poet, standing in the vale of Chamouni, writes his hymn to the "dread mount:"

> "Hast thou a charm to stay the morning star
> In his steep course? So long he seems to pause
> On thy bald, awful head, O sovereign Blanc!
> The Arné and Arveiron at thy base
> Rave ceaselessly; but thou, most awful form!
> Risest forth from thy silent sea of pines
> How silently! Around thee and above
> Deep is the air, and dark, substantial, black,
> An ebon mass; methinks thou piercest it
> As with a wedge! But when I look again,
> It is thine own calm home, thy crystal shrine,
> Thy habitation from eternity;"

it is after his intellect has caught the outlines of that vast dome reaching far up heavenward, girdled with pine trees and crowned with clouds, this religious heart breaks forth in its sweet address to God. Thus faith is an intellect catching, as in a mirror, the image of a Savior and a God, and an eternal realm; and then instantly it becomes a passion bursting forth in all the varied beauty of a happy soul. From reason, or the law of God, Christ calls into service this magnificent mental action to be the basis of his new paradise. Infidelity is the absence of this perceptive power. The magnificent scenery of religion does not open out before it, and in the absence of this ideal world there is no upspringing of any religious passion or sentiment; and a vast realm is blotted from the soul. It was my unhappiness to journey not long since near a little blind girl, riding rapidly through a magnificent country. But while the hills and forests were sweeping by, and while the sun was painting all the western horizon with his tints, blended in infinite delicacy, this beautiful child sat with head bowed toward the floor, the dear heart knowing nothing of the vast pageantry in the heavens, the banners of red and gold floating over the solemn encampments of the woods and the everlasting hills. She was cut off from a measureless world. Infidelity is thus the closing of a sense, and a veiling of a beautiful moral realm; and with the closing of the sense comes the death of a sentiment. Infidelity is the eclipse of a faculty total to the degree of the unbelief, and is hence not so much an insult to God as a natural blight of the heart. Faith is the discovery and enjoyment of a new world — the tendrils by which the vine grasps the oak. Faith saves the soul, therefore, not by any arbitrary decree, not by any form of equivalents or compensation, but by its natural action.

It urges the soul along toward virtue just as the ground presses forward its imbedded germs. The older philosophers made an expression, *natura naturans*, "nature acting naturally," nature in its daily method. In the salvation of the soul, faith is "nature acting naturally." There is nothing arbitrary in the decree. If there were enough truth — truth of morals and redemption — in the Mohammedan or Buddhist system to save the soul, faith would be the law of salvation within those systems. It would be the intellect and the sentiment that would pass through those systems, gathering up their ideas and extracting their passion, hence the Mohammedan has surpassed the Christian in putting to death the infidel. Faith comes into Christianity thus not by an exceptional decree of God, but by the universal law of nature. The mind is so fashioned that its belief is always working out its salvation or destruction. As the ear is always leading the musician forward toward better music, toward a sweet salvation from the rudeness and discords of yesterday, so faith in Christ is always an angel leading the spirit onward, nearer to the condition that knows no sin or sore temptation. When the prophet of God commanded Naaman to go bathe thrice in the river and his disease would be cured, the command was arbitrary. It was not an instance of "nature acting naturally." You may repair to the same river now in sickness, and lo! there is no power in its stream. But when the Bible says, "By faith are ye saved," the words come down from eternity, and belong to the human race in any century and by any shore. As long as the ear may allure the spirit along toward melody, so long will faith unfold in the soul a deeper and more perfect salvation. It is nature, not toiling among rocks and oceans, but toiling in the soul; not a miracle, but a perpetual order of sequence. When God says "Believe and be saved," it is not as it was when He commanded the leader Moses to smite a rock or stretch out a magic rod over the streams of Egypt. That was an isolated command. It was spoken for a day. When the command of faith was spoken, it was spoken in the eternity of the past for the endless years to come. As the idea of decrees does not originate in Christianity but falls into it from the human mind, which always must think that God has decreed all things, and as the difficulty of free-will finds its origin not in the Bible but in the mind itself, so salvation by faith is not a creation or invention of the New Testament, but is a law that has pushed its way up into the Testament from the realm without. In our Oregon coast one finds a hundred miles inland a flood beating along between walls of mountain height, wide, deep and dark. But you taste the water, and lo! it is from the sea. There is an ocean far westward, and this is only a channel cut by its mighty pulsations in the ages past. That faith seen in the New Testament is an arm of a broader, deeper sea. The nature of the human mind, the perpetual laws of God, are a great ontside ocean, one wave of which has worn its way inward toward the manger and tomb of Bethlehem, and instead of faith's being an arbitrary decree passed in the New Testament, it was the basis also of the religion of Socrates or Aurelius.

In the transformation of the soul, two things are at once perceived to be desirable: (1) a new form of industry, and (2) a new form of being, called by theologians *good works*, and a *new heart.* But not aspiring to the honors of theologians, let us not affect their terms, but content ourselves by saying that our safety demands a better industry and a better soul. We must *be* and *act* like Christ. Our industry in traffic, in the arts, in the pursuit of pleasure, is perhaps sufficiently great; but in a moral world capable of virtue and vice, life and death perpetual, an activity is needed of a holier nature. If this world were only a workshop, all might remain as it is; but being a realm of mind and heart, capable of great sin and great sorrow, capable of great virtue and blessedness, and being a vestibule of immortal life, it demands an industry of a peculiar kind, holy, self-denying, and affectionate. The education and christianization of the world are accomplished by the toil of one for another. Your Christianity is handed to you by your friends of yesterday. Your hymns and prayers, your music and your church structure, your taste, your language, were all wrought out for you by loving hearts that are now dead. You are the work of the past. As each child that now plays in its, tenth year, speaking a language, singing a song, revealing a refinement, is only a result of a mother's care and solicitude, so the Christianity of your heart or your age is only a work wrought by hands gone from earth long ago. Each new life is born out of past works, as a rose's bloom is the color of the light that fell upon it in the days that will never come back. Salvation, therefore, is the result of a holy industry. As the coral rocks, rising to the surface of the tropic sea, are the result of a myriadic life, active through long centuries, so salvation comes to its grandeur in this age by help of myriadic praying and singing lips buried now beneath time's old wave, and forgotten in its oblivion. By works of others are we thus saved. The impulse of this grand Christian industry is, faith in Christ as the soul's Savior. It has always been the power that has carried the Pauls over the Ægean, or the pioneer

Methodist to the wilds of America. It has been the earthquake force that has heaved up from a bitter sea a continent of unfading flowers and perpetual spring. Each heart busy in any pursuit, moves by a natural impulse. You know what the love of pleasures does; and you know what is accomplished by what the Latin poet calls "accursed love of gold." Beneath all activity lies an impulse, a motive. Under that vast movement called salvation — that movement which to-day gathers the Laplander to a worship, and makes the Sandwich Islands join with the angels in sacred song; beneath that movement which to-day is the best glory of all civilization, under this vast renewal of the heart — lies faith in Christ, the impulse of all this profound action. The least trace of infidelity lessens the activity; unbelief brings all to a halt, and damns the soul, not by arbitrary decree, but by actually arresting the best flow of its life. Unbelief is not an arbitrary but a natural damnation. Faith in the Infinite Father, faith in Christ the Savior, faith in a life to come, lifts the world up as though the direct arms of God were around it drawing it toward His bosom. It is God in a law. You have seen, out in the summer fields, the beautifully-woven spider's web, with the morning dew glittering upon it, as though its threads were strung with beads of gold. But, suddenly it trembles in every delicate fiber. The builder of it—the little owner of the lace-work—has moved out, and, quick as lightning, all the labyrinth of silk vibrates like a harp-string. Society is spread out like this spider-web. Its lace-work lies over continents, and the decorations of mind and soul hang upon it more gorgeous than any dew-drop beads of gold. Into this tracery are woven the strings of every heart that has lived or is living. But it is a poor dead fabric so far. But, at the first footfall of Christian faith, this vast net-work trembles all over with life, and, becoming as it were harp-strings, breaks forth into a divine melody. Without faith, life is a desert; with faith, a garden of fruit and flowers.

I said that in salvation two things are desirable, a new industry and a new being. We have alluded to the new industry that comes by faith. The idea of a new being will need only a moment's thought. You know of the fabled changes of the chamelion, that it assumes the color of the leaf or rock on which it sleeps; but it is no fable that the heart assumes the color of the soul nearest to it, not in space, but in love. The Mohammedan child assumes the character of that mother who leads it to look to the sacred city and say, Allah. It is thus the world through. The young men of Athens who in love gathered about the feet of Socrates, were changed into his likeness, and he was condemned to death that the public transformation might be arrested. Thus are we all modeled by some character standing above us in reality or by the judgment of our affection. By itself alone each heart is a blank. The soul attached to Jesus Christ by this faith, which is both an intellect and a passion, is gradually transformed into His likeness, and step by step draws near to that salvation found in perfect virtue. In the face of St. John and St. Paul and upon the foreheads of the Marys one may easily see the likeness of Jesus, not in full splendor, but as in the early summer morning one may see the coming day in gentle outline, a radiance in the East. Thus faith is perpetually elaborating a new being, is separating the heart from its yesterday of sin, and bearing it toward its morrow of holiness, a law helped into action by a miracle, but yet a law. No other grace could so save the soul. Charity may do much. It softens the heart and drags along a train of virtues; but it is limited by the horizon of this life. Voltaire and Paine were both beautiful in charity toward the poor, but that virtue seems inadequate. And, of the highest form of charity a religious faith is the best cause, and hence charity must take the place not of a leader but of one that is led. Even penitence is a poor "saving grace" compared with faith, for penitence is not a perpetual impulse but only a regret.

It looks downward. It is not a grand battle cry, but a solemn requiem, not a Gloria but a Miserere. Repentance is herself only the accident of a day. When sin ceases it shall cease. It is not the perpetual impulse of a long life. Repentance would crush the soul did not faith come with its wide horizon, reaching beyond this life and revealing a world where there will be no sin and no regrets. Faith is the normal state of a sinless soul, a youth permeating all the hours from cradle to grave. Other ideas of Christianity fade before it. Baptism, Arminianism, Calvinism, play a poor part within the soul compared with the incessant beating of this wave. The doctrines of penitence, communion, and charity are the satellites only of this star, and are carried around by this great planet as decorations upon the outer border of her garments. As our central sun is equal to millions of such worlds as this earth, as fifty millions of our moon could be poured into it, so faith in Jesus is a central sun into which we could empty all the countless articles of the one thousand sects. It is said that in some of the Scotch churches the articles of study and belief have reached the thousands, but into the one doctrine of belief in Christ as seen in St. John or Magdalen one could empty all the floating star-dust of this Scottish heavens, that dust-cloud having only in past ages concealed this Sun of the gospel sky.

Not only is the individual soul borne to salvation by this influence, but by it all the conditions and generations of men are cast into a profound unity or brotherhood. Not only in mathematics is it true, but also in spiritual things, that things similar to the same things are similar to each other. The world looking up to Christ and becoming like Him is brought into harmony within itself, and the distinctions of wealth, of class, of age, of nation, of sect, are obliterated by the great spiritual oneness of the deepest sentiment. Men are all equal when something raises them up above the distinctions of gold, of furniture, of office, and places them amid the things of the soul. Brotherhood is always created by a dominant sentiment which joins in the great and annihilates in the small. A family circle in a palace or cottage, is cast into sweet unity not by age, for one is silver-haired and one is in the cradle; not by learning, for one is in middle life, full of wisdom, and one is in life's morning, full of inexperience; not by genius, for one is brilliant, another slow of thought; but by a bond of love that runs through all hearts. Home is thus created by a single feeling of love. Thus faith in Christ obliterates the accidental distinctions of earth and makes the tears of a slave and the diadem of a king come in one instant to the dust, to be alike forgiven and forgotten. That likeness to Christ is a transfiguration of earth, so that slave and king appear in the same shining garments.

St. Pierre, in one of his books, describes the return to France of a ship that had for months been beating about among storms in the southern seas. On a certain morning, land was cried from the mast-head. Passengers and crew gathered upon deck in suspense, and forgetting to eat or even fully to dress, they awaited in silence the unveiling of the coming shore. Vague outlines were seen which almost broke the heart by their equal resemblance to either mountain or cloud. After hours that seemed days, the lookout cried, "FRANCE! FRANCE! *It is France.*" The scene that followed illustrates the uniting power of a deep sentiment; for in that hour of joy all took each other by the hand. They kissed their own and each others' children, the storm-beaten captain shook hands with his crew, and the richest gifts passed from high to low. All the miserable distinctions of humanity faded before that blessed vision of the beloved land. Thus the great sentiment of faith in Jesus Christ has power to obliterate poverty or sorrow, rank and bondage, shackles and crowns, and to reveal a human race standing heart to heart. They come up to-day from all paths of life; in all the long centuries past, from all nations they come; and in the future of this world the nations will come, and all looking out on a far-off coast, their voice has been and shall be one, but it is not — "It is France," "It is- France," but IT is Heaven. IT is Heaven. The storms are all over, and we all, led by faith into one heart, are on the shores of Fatherland;

With joyful eyes
The spirit lies
Beneath the walls of Paradise.

ST. JOHN.

SERMON XIV.

ST. JOHN.

IN order that the words of any writer may be held in their true estimate, it is desirable that as much as possible be known of the mind and heart uttering them. The sayings of a Franklin or a George Fox are reinforced by a remembrance of their simplicity and integrity. The same words coming from a thoughtless, shallow character, and from a sober, deep nature, seem to bear within them the littleness of the one voice or the greatness of the other. The books or orations, or poems of a man go forward, for the most part, attended by his character or reputation. If particular words were spoken by a hypocrite, they are worthless, if spoken by a deeply sincere heart, they are valuable.

On account of this close association of a man's words with his character, we should divide our time between the study of doctrines and of the men who announce them. Such a course is due the words and the author, and is due ourselves, since the study of a character unfolds better the meaning of his language to our own mind.

This is our apology for asking you to-day to think, not of some doctrine, but of a man. A more profound respect for an old saint may win from your hearts a deeper respect for his ideas.

John is one of the most influential of New Testament writers. Others may declare Paul to surpass him in affecting religious conduct and thought. In the absence of any method of weighing these two great apostles, we can only express our judgment, that of our land and age St. John is the better exponent, and hence, in its confines, the more influential. Our century, in its extreme love for man, and in its hunger for a religion of sentiment, seems to find its best exponent in the disciple who gave himself up to a friendship with the Savior, and whose favorite advice was, "Children, love one another." There have been ages not far away, that loved most the Mosaic writings. These were the ages of severe government, and of union of church and state. There have been also theological times which have given most of their study and love to the more logical writings of St. Paul; but coming to an era of benevolence and equality, and an era when not only leading minds are to be considered, but when we must admit into the word man all the community of men, women and children, we find St. John to be just now a favorite herald between God and Society.

What we call the public is made up of different elements in different times. Once it was made up of royal families, and then the plays of Shakspeare were full of royal pageantry. Such an age loved most the Old Testament. Passing by these details, when we now speak of society, we do not mean the learned nor the royal, but also we include women, children, and the choice of the times is affected by the choice of all these new hearts and voices. The public demand, made up of these new elements, being wider and more human than ever before, it is best gratified by the affectionate and more universal words of St. John and his Master. John carried in his bosom a model human heart — a heart that finds more parallels in the New World than any other kind of character could secure. When a mind is only philosophic it attracts only philosophers; when it is profound, it attracts only the deep-thinking; when it is only romantic, it appeals to those whose feelings surpass their judgment. But St. John revealed so many attributes that he draws to-day not any one class so much as a whole generation. His gospel sets out in a deep spirit of philosophy. As it advances it passes readily to argument, to simple biography, to sentiment, to poetry, to an overflowing love. He was thus most human, revealing in himself all the cardinal attributes of humanity.

It would seem that the parents of John were in such temporal circumstances that his opportunities for education and reading were as good as any in the country. That he availed himself of his opportunities is evident from his skill in the Greek language, and from his partial acquaintance with the Greek philosophy. His gospel, his letters, and his apocalypse betray at once a reader, a thinker and a poet. The Revelation is a poem just like that of Dante or Milton, his gospel is a selection of what was most divine and valuable in the career of Christ.

But in order to know what education was in that day, it is necessary for you to recall the splendid Greek and Roman world that lay around this gifted young man. The Greek language is still almost an unsurpassed tongue. Eighteen hundred years have added only a small area to the scope of that vast speech. There is scarcely a question of the present day discussed that was not reviewed by the Greek thinkers and stowed away in their manuscripts. Their essays upon education, upon health, upon art, upon amusements, upon war, read almost as though they were written yesterday. Even that question which seems our own, the creation and property of this generation, Whether woman should vote and follow manly pursuits, is all fully discussed in Plato's "Ideal Republic." Remember the poetry also of that speech; remember that nearly all the modern streams seem to have flowed down from that Helicon, and you can then recall the circumstances amid which the apostle John built up his character and amassed his information.

Opening his gospel, we behold the Greek spirit passing over to the service of the Christian religion — "In the beginning was the Word." That Greek term which we translate Word had long been upon the tongues of scholars. Its meaning was always somewhat hidden. It seems to have represented the Supreme Being out upon an errand of mercy, or creation, as light flies away from the sun. It is that Light before which darkness flees; that Life before which death retreats. It is indefinable and inconceivable. Yet, John saw this *Logos* entering the human body as light seems to rush into the eye and sound into the ear. It dwelt among us, and we beheld its glory, full of grace and truth.

Matthew and Luke begin the life of Jesus at the human cradle. Mark omits all the childhood, and opens his record with the adult Savior coming down into Galilee. These three were simple biographers like a Tacitus, an encyclopedist; but John, reared in the school of mysticism and sentiment, sweeps right by the cradle in Bethlehem, and sees the Logos come down out of the deep eternity. The truth is, John's gospel is not so much a biography as an essay, such as has since come to a high mission in literature. He did not attempt the part of a chronicler so much as of a devotee. Passing by the details that had been given by ordinary historians, he came to a more delightful task — that of grouping the characteristics of Jesus so far as they moved about certain centers, and so far as they pleased his own devoted spirit. To have said all about the Savior would have consumed all the life of John; and, as he states, with a beautiful extravagance, the world itself would not have contained the books. It was his privilege and necessity to be simply eclectic, and cull flowers from a field too vast for his full harvesting. In such treatises as Guizot's Life of Calvin and St. Louis, there is only a grouping of great attributes or great events. All minor events are passed by, not only because too many to admit of mention, but because they would cumber both writer and reader, and conceal the valuable ideas. In order for us to perceive anything well, it is essential that other objects be banished from our sight, that the soul may concentrate itself upon the single point. The poet Cowper would not willingly have composed his verses in the market-place, nor could Murillo have painted his spiritual pieces at the city's gate. The first wish of the soul in its responsible offices in life is, that it may be permitted to concentrate its powers upon the task before it, for the hour or for life. But literature also is an art. Indeed, all the parts of life are so many arts. And as the oration or the essay passes by the multiplicity of detail, that the mind may enjoy the pleasure and profit of a single clear and deep view, so the gospel of John brushes away the details, and sets forth a few sublime truths in a clear, powerful light. Hence, it is an Essay upon Christ, like Guizot's sketch of St. Louis, rather than a biography for the archives of the historian.

Christ is not seen in childhood. All those eventless years of the flesh are passed by, that the mind may think of the Logos that came out of the infinite beginning. Joseph and Mary, the decree that all the world should be taxed, the manger, the wrath of Herod — the flight into Egypt, all fade before the eye that desires to see nothing else but a great Light coming in from the East to light the hearts of men.

The Jesus of St. John is first shown to us with a divine spirit descending like a dove upon Him. The first human voice that greets him sounds after full manhood has come, and when on the shores of the Jordan the words are uttered — "Behold the Lamb of God who taketh away the sins of the world."

Out of John's soul we see issuing these ideas, Christ the Divine, Christ the Savior, Christ the Intimate Friend. The opening chapter reveals the divinity of John's Master, and the office of Savior is revealed in every page. The method of the salvation is not detailed as fully as in Paul's letters, but the fact that Christ is the Savior of all who shall love Him, is a brilliant doctrine running through the book. But if there be one idea which more than others fills up this fourth gospel, it is that the Jesus formed and forms an inseparable friendship with mortals, and bears them up to heaven as a mother would fly with her children from storm and death. He becomes one with man as the branch is united to the vine. As He and the Father are bound together, so are He and human life. He goes away to prepare a place for His friends, and He will come again and receive them unto Himself; that where He is there they may be also. All those final remarks and prayers which so instruct and cheer the world, come to us through the medium of St. John, because John did not act as a biographer, but as an essayist and as a final reviewer of life. The Sermon upon the Mount does not appear in the fourth gospel, because John was not repeating the biography of Matthew and Luke, but was taking his own view of Jesus with reference to a few salient features in that wonderful character.

By all who hold to the idea of inspiration it is confessed that divine influence in no way sets aside the disposition or personality of the writer. John and Paul and James all looked at their great Master just as freely and independently as any three modern minds would look upon the career of any great recent character. Thus when the career of Oliver Cromwell is sketched by Froude, we expect the landscape to differ from the one painted by Carlyle, and if there were scores of lives of Cromwell, we should have scores of pictures all truthful and valuable, but each one defective.

It could not have been otherwise in the days when the life of the Savior was delineated by those who stood near him in his earthly years. The gospel of John is Christ as seen by a free and deeply marked individual, not by a collector of facts, but by a gifted genius like a Carlyle or a Froude. John's natural drift was toward mysticism. He did not love the first, natural facts. His was not a hard mind like that of a mathematician with a measuring rod in his hand, nor that of a scientist weighing and dissolving and analyzing a grain of earth or ore. What he loved was not the stones and clods at his feet, but the illimitable space above and beyond the dust and the grass. Coming to a shore which a naturalist would investigate geologically, and from which a child would pick up shells, St. John would stand and look far away into the haze where sea and sky meet and defy mortals to separate their world from infinity.

All around human life, around its material, around its friendship, its love, its learning, its beautiful, and its life itself, there is a remote horizon behind which is reposing a better friendship, a better education, a better beauty, a better life, a circle of haze where earth and sky meet. To pass over the clods at our feet and look into that far-off horizon in which the angels that Jacob first saw betake themselves, this is Mysticism. It was necessary that John's mind should behold Christ only in this transcendental life.

As the magnet will gather up only its own kind of dust, as it will not regard the presence of brass or gold or lead, or even diamond dust, but will from all this scattered richness select only its own elements, as if loving its own friends best, so a gifted mind will from the wide universe of truth gather up only the children of its own heart, all else will be passed by, not in contempt, but because there is something dearer beyond. Had Stuart Mill written a review of America, we can perceive what facts he would have passed by, and what other facts would have been deeply looked into by that far-seeing soul. The condition of the poor, the freedom and hopes of woman, the public honor or dishonor, the marriage relation, the education of our children, the motives of virtue, are themes that would have employed the affection and powers of that heart that has recently become dust. Like the magnet he would have grasped all objects kindred to his own being. He would have passed by religion.

But this peculiar relation of a single mind to the whole truth did not begin in the nineteenth century. It began when the human race began; and this gave us old Homer for poetry, and old Euclid for geometry. Out of such a world came St. John, able to see only all that was ideal and tender and immortal in Jesus Christ. Christ's golden promises of paradise, his sympathy with men, his prayers for his children, his heavenly mansions, his divinity, his light and life, at once filled the apostle's mind, and became the impulse of his eloquence. If you will open the book of Revelation, the Apocalypse, you will see the same John painting all things in the color and light of his own specialized character. As Dante by his own peculiar genius and limitations could not treat of Italy, her religion, her pleasures, her sins, her heaven and hell, except in the exalted form of a poem, rolling like alternate music and thunder, so John by his very education and nature could not walk with his Savior, except upon the borders of cloud, and could not state the doctrines of Christianity except in the symbolism of the Apocalypse. If a doctrine of atonement were to be expressed in didactic form, Paul was the mind for that work; but if John comes to the task of unfolding the same atonement, he beholds some white-robed angels entering paradise, and hears a voice saying, "These are they who have come up from great tribulation, and have washed their robes and made them white in the blood of the Lamb." John argued little; he simply gazed. With him religion was not an inference but a passion. He did not argue for a future life as this age argues. He looked up and saw a holy city coming down from God out of heaven. He saw a pure river of water of life, as clear as crystal, proceeding out of the throne of God and the Lamb. The Holy Spirit can inspire a poet as easily as a historian. There are no prophecies of literal events in the Apocalypse, any more than there are in Tasso or in Tennyson or in Whittier. There is though a poetic soul educated in the Greek school, that school which gave mankind the most intense poetry and the deepest thought; such a soul, seen in every verse of the Apocalypse, smiting upon the facts of Christianity and making them send forth music like a lyre swept by a skillful hand. What Dante was to Italy, John was to Christianity, only in John the divine assisted the human. When Paul has said "we shall all appear before the judgment seat of Christ," he has stated a cardinal truth of Christianity; but when this idea passes from logical Paul to the mystical John, it becomes clothed with its richest drapery, and amid the breaking of seals and the sounding of trumpets and rolling thunders, a vast multitude pour along toward the Great Judge, and beg the overhanging rocks and mountains to cover them from his wrath.

The difference between the gospel of Matthew and the apocalypse of John, is the difference between a history and a gallery of art — the difference between a simple sound and a symphone. Paul said the gospel was to be carried to every nation, just as language and all truth are carried; but in the brain of John this idea became external, and was seen as an angel flying over the earth, saying with a loud voice, "Fear God and give glory to him." For us to inquire the meaning of the seven seals, and to inquire whether Rome be not the "Babylon," would be for us to seek the "Deserted Village" of Goldsmith or the "Beulah Land" of John Bunyan.

When we have said that John was a mystical poet, we have not said that he was less truthful than writers more prosaic. Poetry is often truth carried to its highest expression. Prose is often unable to express an idea. The meaning of the word "God" defies prose, and hence we resort to the poetry of Coleridge or Derzhaven.

"Oh thou eternal one whose presence bright."

Prose will define the word "home" for you in its poor fashion; but if you wish to approach nearer the truth you must fly to the poetry of "Home Sweet Home," and call in also the aid of the still better music. Prose will inform you of death, but if you wish to perceive more of the reality you will have to fly to Bryant's Thanatopsis or to the elegy of Gray in the solemn churchyard.

Poetry is the transfiguration of such ideas as are too lofty for prose. Prose is too narrow in its scope. It can present the truth of law, of science, of history, of theology, but not of religion. A drum will beat a simple, sweet sound, and keep time also, but when the sound would assume the form of music, it demands the many strings and gradations of the harp. So truth, when in the realm of affection or hope or faith or bliss, asks for some more adequate instrument, it rises to the magnificent imagery of the poetic, and pours out there a revelation of itself impossible in the vale beneath.

In the mysticism and imagination of this beloved disciple, I behold, therefore, only the deepest form of inspiration. In his grand, outer horizon we see most clearly the tints, at least, of a sun that is shining in an eternal world, but forbidden of God to throw its full light across the valley of death. The gospel of John, the letters of John, the apocalypse of John, are doubtless the highest and truest form of religion we will ever find on these mortal shores. He, of all the sacred writers, most leads us upward to "where the earth recedes and disappears."

In the natural world, we perceive that the Creator has prepared a golden bed into which, every evening, the sun sinks. Oh! how the classics did love to speak of this dreamy, golden couch. But God loves the human heart more than he loves the stars. Hence, the Savior came. St. John points out to us the beautiful horizon where the soul goes down. And when our friends who have loved God die; when a humble child or a Christlike statesman; when beautiful youth or venerable manhood — bids farewell to earth, and our tears fall upon their dust, we behold best in John's Gospel and Dream the golden couch that receives into its peace these stars sinking down from the sky of this life.

IMMORTAL LIFE.

SERMON XV.

IMMORTAL LIFE.

"For he is not a God of the dead but of the living, for all live unto him."—*Luke 20 : 38.*

THE best evidence of a future life that can be reached by reason alone comes from a contemplation of God rather than from the desires or nature of man. But the trust in immortality comes to different persons by different paths, so that one mind cannot mark out for another the best path to this great hope. Were the evidences of a future existence gathered up in the form and quantity of all times, they would form a library, not only of great extent, but of great variety of thought. Philosophy, poetry, science have their paths of argument in this great field. In our thought, this morning, we need not be limited by the special argument of the text, but may come to that single thought after having expressed some general views upon the interesting topic. One reason why we may go at last for our hope to the contemplation of God is found in the fact that the material world comes short of indicating, in any manner, the perpetual life of man. The tree which in winter casts all its foliage; the flowers which, having been cut down by the frost, bud again in the spring, are only poetic illustrations of a human resurrection, but do really suggest nothing of argument, for this tree and this blossoming do not die in this falling of leaves. When, in subsequent years, the tree has really died and entered upon its decay, as man dies and decays, it sends forth no more leaves ever again. Its organism dissolves and passes into the life of other forms of organism. Thus nowhere does the material kingdom fling out a hope of immortality to man as an individual, but only to man as a class. The apple and peach which ripened last autumn will never ripen again, and hence they only indicate to us that other fruits will adorn our fields a hundred years hence as they adorned them a hundred years ago. Thus all organized nature indicates, not a perpetual life for the individual, but only for the class.

The fact that the material world argues only in favor of endless succession is probably a cause of the infidelity which so often springs up from a devotion to the study of natural science. Nature is full of death for all individual life from the humblest to the highest. The tree, the fish, the insect, the great mammals dying are all confessed to have ceased to exist. The species rolls on, like a succession of waves beating against a shore, but where each special wave comes but once in the long, long storm. When students of nature have spent life amid this absolute death of the individual and absolute continuance of only the species, it is easy for many of them, coming to look upon man, to feel that he too is only an organism of material, wonderful indeed and superior, but yet only dust organized for a brief career. It is not my design to state here that it is the habit of scientific minds calmly to reject the idea of a second life, but that their studies oppose a deep love for or any confidence in the doctrine. It does not live in their soul as it lives in the feelings of those who study the spiritual side of the universe more than they study the nature which, in their sight, is always resolving itself into dust. The number of persons who deny that there is any future life is no doubt very small, for no one can be positive regarding any point of which he simply knows nothing, but the number of those who do not hold this doctrine with any confidence is, I fear, painfully great. It is to be inferred not so much from any loud words as from their silence or from the doubts with which the grave seems clouded when they venture to speak. The silence of lofty intellects comes not always from an aversion to topics that seem too religious, but often from doubts which make them unwilling to associate their eloquence with what may be only a dream. In my own intercourse with my fellowmen I have found the naturalists least wedded to the idea of an immortal life, and that the best friends of the hope are to be found among those who are students of justice — the lawyer, the judge, the legislator, or those busy in philanthropy or education — persons living in presence of the soul. The naturalist so deeply loves and studies matter in all its wonderful combinations between the ether that makes worlds and the electricity which makes a dead pulse to beat, that to him, absorbed in such phenomena the human mind seems only a flame created by the chemical combustion of food. If you will read Dr. Carpenter upon the brain, you will for the hour feel that man is nothing but a retort into which various elements are mingled and heated, until a poem or an oration or an anecdote is the result.

In all this analysis of vital action there is much truth, but in order to reach the best conception of man, it seems best to begin the inquiry from another standpoint, that of first falling in love with the idea of soul, in love with the theory of spirit, and then from that prepossession set forth to investigate the particular form of spirit called man. If it is lawful for the naturalist to give his affections to material forms and thus, in his prejudice for his world, reach the conclusion, at last, that mind is only the effervescence of a chemical cauldron, it is equally lawful for you and me to be prepossessed with the charms of spirit and to reach the feeling that flesh is only the chariot in which this angel of life rides in these and upon other shores. It is well known that the mind shapes its material form. The face of a Webster is nobler, the forehead higher, the eye brighter, and the brain larger than are those features or faculties in a Sioux Indian, and it must be so, because in Webster there is a mind and soul which have for two thousand years been busy shaping the tabernacle of dust. In order to believe well in a future beyond, it seems essential that one make the assumption of spirit a starting-point, and then the whole material world becomes its servant, or its arena, or decoration; but if, with Huxley and Darwin, we begin with the assumption of matter, there seems nothing to throw us over across the dividing ocean, and we must remain on the shore of dust, and hence death; for move to and fro as material does from wild rose to full-leafed rose, from ape to man, it always brings us at last only to dust. There is no immortal rose, however full-leafed it may become. Death is its destiny. To get over this tomb of roses and of man it is essential that a spirit be assumed, a God, an essence differing from the vital action of the heart or of the roots of the wild flowers. In this study of man, after we assume that he possesses a spirit, the text enters with its single thought that God is not a God of dead souls, but of living ones. There is no manifest reason for supposing a soul made in such a divine image to be only an ephemeral creature, going quickly to nothingness, thus making God the father of the dead rather than of the living. All the reasons for creating such a being as man remain for continuing his existence. If when the Creator had formed such a universe as lies around us here, of which our system is as a grain of sand upon an infinite shore, He finally concluded to make man a race to inhabit one or more stars of the universe, a race in the divine image, a human life of a few years would seem wholly unworthy of such a boundless material realm; for we cannot master its truths nor taste its happiness in any three-score year career. Your children have shown their divine nature, have revealed their intelligence, have spoken a few words, have rejoiced in a few spring times, and have gone hence, leaving you heart-broken over a speechless form. A brief career is thus not in harmony with the immense universe in which this life begins and of which man is unquestionably the highest order of being.

That man is of the highest order of being would appear from the following comparison of qualities:

The Creator must possess the following attributes—being, wisdom, power, holiness, justice, goodness, and truth. A glance at man reveals at once the same attributes, and hence man is in quality the highest order of created beings. But if man's life varies from a day to a few years only, then he has everything except being. He has the attributes of a God, and the arena of a brute or an insect. The magnificence of these attributes ought to presuppose a magnificence of being. When God hung out the planet Jupiter he gave it an orbit worthy of its gigantic proportions. It sweeps about a circle whose diameter is a thousand millions of miles, and yet it traverses all this long journey in the light and verdure of perpetual spring. It must be that when God made the soul he gave it an orbit, a being commensurate with its mental and spiritual endowments, and not a tomb a few steps from its cradle. The immense endowments of man implies an immense arena of time; and coming as he does from a Creator who is inconceivable as to his immensity, there is no more reason for supposing that man was made for an early grave, than that the sun or the planet Jupiter was made simply for a passing hour. Reason teaches us that an immense equipment for life presupposes an immense life. As vast foundations indicate a palace or temple, expected to endure, so the human mind and heart reveal foundations that were not laid for the pitching of a tent, but for a fabric worthy of the deep and wide base.

But the proportions of the intellect are no more significant than those of the heart. Indeed, when we perceive the imperfections of intellect, of logic, and of knowledge, and that the highest learning is but a step along the infinite path, one might almost accept of eternal death as being the best end of such intellectual despair, but of the heart no such humiliating words can be spoken. Its love is immense though its knowledge and logic may come short. The love of a mother, a father, our love of friends, of nature, of beauty, this is all genuine and free from the humility attached to the pursuit of truth. Newton and Locke and all philosophers may mourn that they come so far short, but they cannot mourn that their heart's love came short of reality. The mother, the child might deplore the poor progress of their intellect, but as for their heart it rises like an unfettered bird. Love prefigures eternity. And hence, when we see friends bury their nearest and best loved ones in the very morning of the soul's attachment, we feel that earthly love, having earth only for its arena, is a sublime star without an orbit — a deep foundation with no superstructure. Human love with no basis except this life is a wonderfully fantastic creation, for more than three-fourths of the objects some of you have loved have been long hidden away in the tomb. Oh what armies of loved children have been laid into the grave out of mothers' arms! Oh what armies of young friends stand back of us whose faces we shall never see here, and which we never saw except just long enough to catch a burning picture in our heart, and are these forever gone? Then love in the soul of man is only a fantasy; this, too, with man, the highest order of being conceivable next to God; and this, too, in a world full of God's immensity and tenderness. I shall not believe that God is vast in the orbit and bulk and numbers of the stars, and is small only in the gifts and arena of the spirit.

Astronomers tell us that the motion of the earth has not probably varied in a million years. They have no figures for expressing the age of the sun. All is wonderful except man. Endowed with a mind like Deity, endowed with a heart like the divine heart, he is doomed to a grave before his powers have reached even a partial action. Thirty-three years sweeps away all this human pageant. If this be true there is nothing so imperishable as a stone, there is nothing so contemptible as a divine soul. The oak tree will live a thousand years, and thus will see thirty generations of men pass away. There are oaks in England in whose shade children have played, and kings and queens have paused to rest, in the fifteen hundred years gone. The white elephants of India live a century, thus surpassing that being whom we behold endowed with reason, memory, hope, love, and religion. If man has no life beyond, then we perceive this being taken away from the highest order of earth, and bestowed upon the oak of the forest, or the dumb brute of India. This reason must deny and must feel that man must surpass the brute world by a life upon another shore. *There* is to be found an arena of time adequate to the lofty endowment of mind and heart which man possesses.

The resurrection of the soul may be inferred not only from the grand quality of its attributes but from their method of growth. If man came into this life with full powers, and for seventy years shone with full light all the while without any loss, then the mind might be perplexed, but when we observe that through all this life the mind only begins to acquire wisdom and knowledge and virtue, and finds its best days only when the hair begins to whiten for the grave, we must conclude that if the tomb be the end then there is too much preparation, and too little for which to prepare, an education without a destiny. At the lowest estimate twenty-five years of life are consumed in building up a common education and stable character; but the average of human life is thirty-three years. These facts resolve human life into a grand preparation for something that is never to take place, a long temptation, and study, and repentance, and prayer, and self-sacrifice in order that it may become annihilated in the grave. Life is by all confessed to be a school, for we perceive our fellow-men to be undergoing great transformations, and we all experience great transformations in its long bright or weary hours. But if this school opens its door at last upon death, and graduates its children into the tomb alone, what a mockery is our long and for the most part sorrowful tuition. In order for reason to reach such a destiny of man it is necessary to divest the Creator not only of kindness but also of the honor of intelligence. The quality of the human attributes and the long period demanded by their development here, point out therefore a life of broader extent than is to be seen in these three-score years. The reasons for man's existence here all continue in favor of an existence hereafter. If the work of this life is to build up character there should be some place for that character to repair to better than the sepulcher. I do not believe that such a soul as that of St. Paul, woven out of life's love and sorrows, ran out in the blood that drenched the block at Rome, where his eyes closed in death. I do not believe that God made any of these sublime human characters simply for a burial either in the tomb of a country churchyard or in the Abbey of Westminster. There is nothing in the nature of man that justifies any other outlook than that broad open sky called immortality.

Did you ever take your pencil and estimate how many human beings a single star or planet might support? If you will do so, you will find that there is one of our planets that would support upon its bosom all the inhabitants that have ever lived upon the earth in its historic six thousand years. With a population only as dense as that of France, our largest planet would furnish homes for all the beings that have ever lived on our small but beautiful star. But what is one planet to the millions of worlds that deck the sky? Earth is the humblest of stars. Oh, man! God's universe has as much room for his children all living, as for his children all dead; as much room for their life and love and joy as for their dust. And this brings us at last to the full light of the text. Moving about for the hour in its twilight, we emerge now into its fuller, sweeter beam. "God is not a God of the dead, but of the living, for all live unto Him." God is not a being rich in the tombs of those whom He once loved, and who once loved Him, rich in sepulchers of Abraham, Paul, John, all the Marys, Luther, and the Wesleys. He is not a God of a vast world covered with graves of noble men and dear children. Oh, no! all live unto Him. Death is nothing else than the limit of human gazing. Man sees a cloud not visible to the Almighty. The river of death rolls not before the eye of God, but the gaze of man. "UNTO HIM ALL LIVE." The theory of man's mortality makes God the owner of a great burial-place, which offers no hymn, no prayer, no praise, to a God of love and wisdom — nothing but silence and solitude. Earth is only a tomb; and if there be no heaven, God is the divine owner of a vast burying-ground. For you remember what our great Bryant sung for us in our childhood. He says, earth is nothing but a sepulcher:

"The hills,
Rock-ribbed and ancient as the sun, the vales
Stretching in pensive quietness between,
The venerable woods, rivers that move
In majesty, and the complaining brooks
That make the meadows green, and poured round all

> Old ocean's gray and melancholy waste,
> Are but the solemn decorations all
> Of the great tomb of man. The golden sun,
> The planets, all the infinite host of heaven
> Are shining on the sad abodes of death
> Through the still lapse of ages. All that tread
> The globe are but a handful to the tribes
> That slumber in its bosom. Take the wings
> Of morning and the Barcan desert pierce,
> Or lose thyself in the continuous woods,
> Where rolls the Oregon, and hears no sound
> Save his own dashing, yet the dead are there."

Now, my friends, all this desolation, all this rain of human tears, and sighing of autumnal winds, is a solemnity that confines its sorrow to man alone. As for God, earth is not a vast tomb, but a vast mount of resurrection and transfiguration.

Out of human tombs the soul is rising like a silvery vapor from the dark sea. To man, living upon the low surface of the earth, the sun goes down and disappears; but this comes to pass from the fact that man's horizon is a small circle fringed by a range of mountains or a sea. But could man dwell in the upper ether he would perceive that the sun does not go down, but pours forth an ocean of light forever. Thus death is a human horizon, where the soul seems to go down to the gaze of mortals. Dark mountains and a vale of shadows intervene; but to God, far above us, looking upon all his stars, and all his angels, and the children of men, the horizon which we call death disappears, and the soul shines always. *Unto Him all live.*

A REASONABLE ORTHODOXY.

SERMON XVI.

A REASONABLE ORTHODOXY.

"**Present your bodies a living sacrifice, holy, acceptable unto God, your reasonable service.**"—*Rom. 12:1.*

THE fact that Christianity is assumed to come from God imposes upon it the obligation of being wonderfully reasonable and just in its demands upon faith and conduct. God is the great ideal of human righteousness, and hence that which comes from Him must pass before us in a justice above the justice of politics or ordinary human action. God is everywhere held forth as a righteousness. How man can be righteous in the sight of Him before whom the heavens are unclean, how man can be just with God, is the great question resting heavily in each consciousness. Compared with divine justice, human estimates of right and wrong are like a child's survey of the ocean, or of the midnight sky. The human family has drawn much of its happiness from the idea that in all their dark hours of slavery, or tyranny, or pestilence, or poverty, there was over them one being who would make no mistakes, but would secure to all the most righteous results. Though the child of God walk through the valley and shadow of death, yet he need fear no evil, for God's support will still comfort him.

Now this infinite justice in some of its applications becomes what is called reasonableness, a branch of justice. That God should be unreasonable is impossible, for under such a confession the whole idea of God disappears. He is nothing unless reasonable. If a master should compel his slave to toil twenty-three hours a day, he would be considered as an unreasonable monster. Of God, therefore, who is the fountain of all the justice which man possesses, perfect reasonableness is a prime attribute.

Assuming, therefore, this quality of the divine being, we ought to expect this infinite intelligence to express itself in the ideas of the Christian religion, for we dare not deduce a religion of nonsense from a being of perfect intelligence. When the poet says:

"I doubt not through the ages one increasing purpose runs,
And the thoughts of men are widened with the process of the suns,"

it is assumed that that "increasing purpose" is not the resolve of a mere despot, but of an immense wisdom and love.

All through the Christian religion, therefore, there may be assumed to exist an intelligence reflecting the image of God, appealing to the intelligence of man. Man being wholly inferior to the Almighty, it will not be possible for this inferior creature to read perfectly the whole eternal purpose, but there will be many a place in the doctrines and the practice of religion where the human reason will perceive the divine purpose. There will be mysteries, but also there will evidently be manifest a great amount of what we call common sense.

St. Paul suggests this line of thought when he beseeches his brethren to bring to the altars of God, not their lambs and doves, but their own bodies, and not to bring them as dead, but as living sacrifices, holy and acceptable, a reasonable service. What God needs is not the death of a lamb or a dove in man's stead, but a devotion of the human heart to His law and His worship, and thus men must bring not some subterfuge, some shadow of religion, but a rational union of the human soul and its Maker. Offerings had served a purpose as shadowing a religion, but they had never been a positive religion. Instead of being an education, they had only been an alphabet Real religion is the state of the mind and soul towards the Creator, and all objects coming between are valuable only so far as they help to this one result. Fully realizing that much in Christianity is perfectly intelligible, and is not simply a command issued out of darkness into darkness, we seem to walk the path of salvation with a better self-consciousness and firmer faith. There is, perhaps, nothing which so retards evangelical Christianity, as the common habit of its pulpit and pew to cry mystery more than is really necessary, and to blind their eyes to reason, as though in confessing reason they were denying the supernatural, and were opening the gates to a flood of Rationalism.

Although much of infidelity has come from the natural wickedness of man, yet it is not to be for a moment denied that much of it has resulted from the extreme unreasonableness of the teachers of religion in all church history. Such were the extravagant statements of doctrine in the past, that in order to find room for their logical powers, scholars and thinkers were compelled to step outside the church. Faith, for example, was once interpreted as being a blind belief, and that the more difficult the thing to believe, the more merit there was in accepting it. To make a doctrine reasonable, was just exactly what the enthusiastic days of faith tried to avoid. To find it incredible seemed the supreme wish. Hence Luther says: "The high perfection of faith is to believe that God is just, notwithstanding by His own choice He renders us necessarily damnable." This single sentence throws a world of light upon that whole age when the most absurd ideas were held by the best men. Holding unreasonable ideas was most valuable, because it showed how faith had triumphed above the poor sinful impulses of the logical faculty. Faith was not a deep friendship for Jesus Christ, but was only an insane acceptance of incredible things. Out of such an era came the race of great skeptics, from Montaigne down to Voltaire, Hume and their schools. Under the calmer skies of the present, wherein faith is not defined as a mania for the improbable, but a devotion to Christ, which fastens the Christian to His cross and life rather than to dark mysteries, such a violent revolt to infidelity would have been almost impossible. Faith is no longer defined as the power to believe God to be just when he damns the innocent, but is only a communion of spirit of man with spirit of Christ, as though an inseparable friendship were binding the human and the divine.

In the old centuries when faith was a grappling with the marvelous, all salvation was secured the moment this belief was reached, and hence salvation was not so much a new holy life as a new credulity, an eclipse of reason.

In our age, faith is a gigantic force; not a form of indifference to all logic, but a kind of presence of Christ which impels along the path of duty and joy and sanctification. It is said by a careful historian that the wonderful stories which grew up in the mediæval church were invented daily in order to bring the children and the common people into this power of belief. The priest related his visions or miracles, so as to force the multitude to believe in the wonderful nearness of either God or Satan, and thus suddenly to find salvation by a belief into which they had been entrapped by a fine artifice. If, for example, your child of ten, or even of fifteen years, should fail to seek its first communion, and fail to confess belief in the reality of your immense religion, you may invent a dream or a vision in which God came to you and unfolded something dreadful, if the child should remain outside of the church, or above all, should reveal any inclination toward some alien sect. Thus to hurry into an intellectual belief, was the first refuge of the soul, and all beyond that was quite insignificant. In the course of human inquiry it was unavoidable that this great scaffolding and framework of credulity, and of a dead belief divorced utterly from a correct life, should fall and drag down part of the unfinished superstructure, and out of the collapse of this folly should come infidelity enough to cover a whole continent. The return of our times toward true Christianity must come from a return to a reasonable creed, not to a rationalism that denies all supernatural events, but to a reason that shall clothe faith, and penitence, and virtue, and all of salvation with the best raiment possible of common sense. Faith is indeed appointed of God to be a legal salvation, but God is the author of wisdom, and hence he gave faith its legal power, because it possessed such a grand natural power.

God might have ordained that all persons who should crawl upon their knees from Paris to Rome, or from the Atlantic to the Mississippi, should be saved, and this would have been evermore a legal salvation; but what would have been the causal relation between such pilgrimages and human energy in all the personal reform and benevolent works of the world? The vilest sinner could have performed the task, and then have lived on in sin; but when God attaches salvation to faith in Jesus Christ, to such a divine friendship, he has set in motion an influence that will help each soul possessing this faith up to a holy living. God made religion reasonable by making prominent in its doctrines a reasonable agency, a great natural force called belief. If God desired to overthrow the everlasting hills, He would not probably ask the gentle wind to blow upon them, or the birds to sing over them, but He would ask the earthquake to open its great bosom and swallow them, as it once withdrew the realm of Atlantis. Thus faith comes into Christianity, not simply by an arbitrary decree, but by an order springing from the reasonableness of God and the nature of man. This faith is a part of the reasonable service demanded by the ideal church, escaped from the worship of superstition and folly.

It is incredible that a God of infinite wisdom should encumber the soul's progress with doctrines arbitrary or absurd. It is not only to be presumed that God desired that His children should reach heaven, but that they should develop their own intellect and spirit on the way. Hence, if God has promulged a religion we may assume beyond question that it will not be divorced from culture and bound to superstition, but will, in every doctrine, be a handmaid of the world's common sense. If reason is confessedly one of the highest attributes of man, it certainly should not be denied the Father in heaven. In the simplest rites of the church, therefore, in the baptism of an infant, or the immersion of an adult, there will be a reasonableness worthy of God above and man beneath. This common sense cannot lie in any saving power such a rite may bring, for water cannot form any part of a spiritual regeneration. Water can no more stand as a part of salvation, than of a classic education, or as a preparation for the bar or the senate. Spiritual changes do not thus come. But if the baptism stands as an *emblem* of a new life that shall otherwise come to the soul, or as a moment when parents make solemn vows before heaven and earth, then the rite passes into its reasonableness and becomes a leaf of the vast intelligence above and beneath. When, therefore, mothers have wept in hopeless agony because a loved child has died unbaptized, they have disgraced their Maker by their tears, for is God a being who could condemn a soul, because it had had no water sprinkled upon its forehead. Is the eternal misery of a soul of so little significance, in the sight of God? Oh! a moment's thought over the sweet reasonableness of the Heavenly Father could dry many eyes that have wept too long and too bitterly.

Passing along over the Christianity of the far-off yesterday, I perceive everywhere that it has ascribed everything to God except the great virtue of common sense. Permit me to illustrate still further this proposition. Take, for example, the sinfulness of man. We all know of this sinfulness, we feel it, we repent of it, we pray for escape from it. How truthfully this idea is expressed all over the Holy Scriptures! One says we are born to trouble as the sparks to fly upward. Another says, "There is none that doeth good; no, not one." Again it is said, "When we would do good, evil is present with us." What a world of truth there is in these statements! There is not even an infidel who will rise up and deny them, for they lie so close to the calmest reason of man. But let the church zealots take hold of these verses and re-express them in the language of an age that loves dark things, and which thinks that the more mystery the more faith, and you have handed the beautiful religion of Christ to the care of almost a raving madness. Contrast with the Bible the old statement of Bishop Beveridge, and he stands for the seventeenth century: "I cannot pray but I sin; I cannot hear or preach a sermon, but I sin; I cannot give an alms or receive a sacrament, but I sin; nay, I cannot so much as confess my sins to God but my very confessions are only aggravations of them;" and you will perceive that such words are only a transfer of the Bible from its sweet reason to the care of human fanaticism; and out of such transfer has rolled upward the cloud of infidelity that darkens the world. Such language not only makes perfect nonsense of religion, but it exasperates the educated heart, and helps divorce Christianity from the public culture. My friends, it becomes us all to tear, not only our own hearts away from such wild statements, but to help pluck such a badge of dishonor from the name of our Father, and from the cross of our Blessed Lord. It is only by this open purifying of the sanctuary, you can make it worthy of the coming generations, issuing from the school-house and from homes of varied culture. There is great goodness in the heart that truly attempts to take its communion, or to repent of its sins; and the good book, compared with which all books are dust, instead of finding sin in repentance, declares there is joy in heaven among the angels over the sinner that repents; whereas, if what Bishop Beveridge said two hundred years ago be true, the angels ought to weep that the sinner is so aggravating his sins by confessing them on bended knee.

Theodore Christlieb, and with him Lecky and Baring Gould, affirms that infidelity is not so much a result of the pretenses of the Bible as of the pretenses of men who have lived long since; and that each extravagant dogma of the church has bred infidels by myriads all around the bad dogma. In a work upon infidelity, a work so powerful and true that it has just been published by the American Tract Society, Christlieb says: "It must be confessed that the church theology of the last century deserves the chief blame for the general apostacy which then began from the ancient faith. Rationalism was right in contending for simple righteousness in opposition to a theoretic orthodoxy."

In all its history the Tract Society has never published a volume so useful, so bold, so impressive.

Now, we all know, my friends, that there is no logic upon the earth that can bring all the ideas of Christianity down to human comprehension, for the finite cannot grasp all the thoughts and plans of the infinite, but in dealing with His reasoning children, it is to be assumed that to a very great degree a religion from God direct will appeal constantly, not to the credulity and superstition of society, but to its calmest judgment, and the more the public culture advances, the more will advance the divine creed, recommending itself afresh to each improving generation. It is only a human religion, such as that of Buddha, or Thor, or Jupiter, that may fear the growth of intelligence, and that may fade as the light of reason dawns, but of a religion from God, given by inspiration, the first distinguishing feature must be that it will reveal its reasonableness as fast as man unfolds his own intelligence, and will become most glorious where there is the most culture. The mediæval Christianity having been disfigured by ignorance and superstition, the subsequent growth of reason had to express itself in infidelity. When a Dante describes hell to mankind, and his frightful pictures become or betray the theology of the church sweeping through Romanism over into Protestantism, and following along until Edwards says, God will dash the sinner down on hells's floor and stamp upon him, then infidelity must follow not simply to save men from such horrors, but to rescue God's blessed name from such unspeakable infamy. In such a hell as Dante's, it is not man that is punished, it is God that is destroyed. From such ideas we must fly to a more reasonable religion, carrying the cross and our holy faith away with us from such a degradation. We must indeed separate forever the righteous and the wicked, but as the drunkard is punished in this world, and as the murderer accepts of his fate, without blaming God, as the soul feels its own wickedness and does not reproach the Creator, so the lost world is a place not where God is seen as a cruel monster, but where the human free-will stands forth in all its divine powers and reveals a self-punishment over which we can almost imagine the Heavenly Father himself to shed tears. Such is the perdition of reason, a place not where the Savior and God become inquisitors, but where the sinner's own will and own heart have woven for himself garments of perpetual sackcloth, and where the tears of sorrow fall not from a malicious decree of God passed from eternity, but fall out of the sinner's own wicked soul and misspent life. Any other view annihilates God.

Thus over almost every idea in the Christian religion, there is lying a drapery of reason fresh from the Being of infinite wisdom, and beautiful to man, the image of the rational God.

It is not rationalism that the world asks for. There are a few minds between Darwin and old Lucretius, which have asked for a full explanation of all phenomena, and which will confess only what they can comprehend. But the human soul the world over loves the mysterious, and bows in sweet humility before the throne of the Invisible. The union of God and man in a Christ, the influence of the Holy Spirit, the doctrine of immortality, all these ideas are just as liable to be welcome a thousand years hence, as they were with the disciples of the first century or the nineteenth. No! Mankind does not ask or crave for a pure rationalism, that will reduce life to a chemical action and heaven to a dream. Mankind will never object to what is sublimely above reason; in fact we all love the sweet mysteries of the skies; but what man will never tolerate, is that his reason should be contradicted and torn all to atoms in his sight. The human mind knows the difference between a mystery and a fraud.

Let us then, my friends, you in your walks of life, and I in mine, go on unfolding as far as possible, the reasonableness of our sublime creed, saying to the outside world, and to our own hearts, how wise is this salvation by faith, how wise is this hope, how rational is this charity, how probable is this Gospel, how appropriate this baptism, how reasonable but how sad is this separation of the righteous from the wicked, —how much like God is yon Paradise!

> "Sure he that made us with such large discourse,
> Looking before and after, gave us not
> That capability and God-like reason
> To fust in us unused."

If, my friends, it was the departure of the old church from the paths of childlike simplicity; if it was her surrender of herself to a career of contempt for the intellect, a career which declared the human will to be like Lot's wife, "a dead pillar of salt" in a volcanic desert, which declared faith to be only an arbitrary salvation, and that the highest act of faith was to believe the most impossible thing, which declared works must be wholly unthought of as pleasing to God, and which, in a word, distorted everything between the creation and the perdition of mankind; if it was this that drove millions into infidelity, then the only hope remaining for combining modern culture and Christianity must be found in coming forward again with the simple, reasonable truth of Jesus Christ. Society will never reject Him, nor His words, nor His hope. The world alienated by the church's credulity must be allured back by its reason; repelled by a flaming picture of God's revenge; it must be persuaded back by a presentation of His most tender justice; driven into unbelief by our narrowness, it must come back by our breadth; cast off by our exclusiveness, it will never return until welcomed by our extreme and unmingled love.

DECLARATION

IN REPLY TO THE

CHARGES OF PROF. PATTON.

DECLARATION.

TO THE MEMBERS OF THE CHICAGO PRESBYTERY:

Called upon in the outset of these proceedings to enter my plea to the charges and specifications presented by Francis L. Patton, I beg permission to submit the following: I object to the charges as too vague and as embracing no important offense; yet, not wishing to raise any technical objections, I enter the plea of "not guilty." I admit the extracts from sermons and writings, but I would ask the Presbytery to consider the entire essays or whole discourses from which the extracts are made. I avow myself to be what, before the late union, was styled a New School Presbyterian, and deny myself to have come into conflict with any of the Evangelical Calvinistic doctrines of the denomination with which I am connected, and I beg permission to enter as a part of my plea the following statements: 1. Regarding my relations to the Liberal Churches. 2. Regarding my relation to the Presbyterian Church. Of these I shall speak in their order.

By way of explaining the quantity of the public offense, I will state that of the fifteen lectures delivered in this city for benevolent purposes, all but two were on behalf of the Evangelical churches, and, in all cases but one, remuneration was declined. Hence the spirit that prompted such lectures must have been not any marked partiality for the so-called Liberal societies. This much as to the quantity of the alleged offense. Upon the quality of the conduct I would submit the following observations:

1. There is no valuable theory of life except that of good-will toward all men. It is only on the basis of a wide friendship any one can live well the few years of this existence, and hence to decline to lecture on behalf of a Unitarian chapel would do more harm to the mutual good-will upon which society is founded, than it would do good to an orthodox theology, or harm to a Liberal creed.

2. If the object of the Evangelical pulpit is to promulge its better truth, it can do so only so far as its ministry reveal a deep friendship toward all mankind, and so far as they unfurl the banner of their own love, while they are presuming to speak of the impartial love of their Divine Master. There remains no longer any power of authority in the pulpit. The time when the civil police drove a halting sinner into the true church

has disappeared, and the modern pulpit must communicate its ideas along the chords of friendship, and he will persuade the most men whose heart can gather up the largest and most diverse multitude into the grasp of its pure affections.

3. But let us come now to the grandest reason why a Presbyterian may express in many ways a kind regard for these so-called Liberal sects. The sin of the "lecture," as charged, must be based upon the assumption that the Unitarian sects are outcasts from God, having no hope in the life to come. The names of Channing, and Elliott, and Huntington, and Peabody, in the pulpits of that sect and the Christ-lives of thousands in the congregations of that denomination, utterly exclude from my mind and my heart the most remote idea that in showing that brotherhood any kindness, I am offering indirect approval to persons outside the pale of the Christian religion and hope. The idea that these brethren are doomed to wrath beyond the tomb I wholly repudiate. It is, indeed, my conviction that they do not hold as correct a version of the Gospel as that announced by the Evangelical Alliance a few years ago, yet I am just as certain that the Blessed Lord does not bestow his forgiveness and grace upon the mind that possesses the most accurate information, but upon the heart that

loves and trusts Him. It is possible, that the venerable Dr. Hodge, of Princeton, holds a more truthful view of Jesus than may be held by the distinguished Peabody, who has just lectured from his Unitarian standpoint before the Calvinists in the Union Theological Seminary, but we can point to nothing in the Bible that would indicate that heaven is to be given to only the one of these two giants who may possess the clearer apprehension of a truth. It may be assumed that God grants the world salvation only on account of the expiatory atonement made by a Redeemer, but that God will grant this salvation to only those who fully apprehend this fact, is an idea not to be entertained for an instant, for this would give heaven only to philosophers, and indeed only to those of this small class who shall have made no intellectual mistake. Looking upon the multitudes who need this salvation, and seeing that they are composed of common men, women, and children who know nothing of the distinctions of formal theology, we cannot but conclude that paradise is not to be a reward of scholarship, but of a loving, obedient faith in Jesus Christ.

When we remember these things, and recall that Dr. Isaac Watts was accused of being a Unitarian, so difficult often is it to perceive the dividing line, we cannot for a moment, place these persons called Unitarians outside the great and generous love of the Savior. I stand ready, therefore, at all times, to express toward these sects a friendship not only human, and wise, and social, but also Christian.

The harmony existing between all these brethren and myself, is not a harmony of views in mind, but a harmony of love in the soul. They each and all know that I differ widely from them, but this they and I know; that only the most gentlemanly treatment in public and private will we all receive always from each other. Much as I love Presbyterianism—a love inherited from all my ancestors—if on account of it, it were necessary for me to abate in the least my good-will toward all sects, I should refuse to purchase the Presbyterian name at so dear a price.

The second point to be alluded to was my relations to Presbyterianism. A distinction evidently exists between Presbyterianism as formulated in past times and Presbyterianism *actual.* A creed is only the highest wisdom of a particular time and place. Hence, as in States, there is always a quiet slipping away from old laws without any waiting for a formal repeal, as some of the old statutes of Connecticut are lying dead, not by any legal death, but by long emaciation and final neglect of friend and foe; so in all formulated creeds, Catholic or Protestant, there is a gradual, but constant, decay of some article or word which was once promulged amid great pomp and circumstance. And yet no church is willing to confess its past folly and repeal the injurious or untrue. All, Catholic and Protestant, simply agree to remain silent.

In the Presbyterian Confession of Faith, there are about two hundred formulas of truth, or supposed truth. It is a wonderful argument in favor of this compendium, that not one-tenth of these have been found false to the Bible or false to the welfare of society. To designate these two hundred as Calvinism is a gross injustice, for they are almost all valuable truths, common to all churches, and gathered up from the sacred page.

But from a few statements out of this large number, the *actual* Presbyterian Church has quietly passed away. Conventions cannot be called every few years to amend or repeal some one article. It would entail endless debate and expense, and perhaps promote wide discord, thus to call, from time to time, a new Westminster Assembly. As the Christian world avoids a revision of the translation of the Bible because of the tumult such a new version would probably create among the sects, so each particular church postpones as long as possible any formal modification of its historic statements of doctrine. But meanwhile individual minds cannot be slaves; they cannot suspend the use of their judgment and best common sense. Hence, unable to revoke any dangerous idea by law, the Presbyterian Church permits its clergy to distinguish the *actual* from the church *historic.* To the Presbyterian Church actual I have thus far devoted my life, giving it what I possess of mind and heart.

Chief among the doctrines which our church has passed as being incorrect, or else an over-development of Scriptural ideas, are all those formulas which looked toward a dark fatalism, or which destroy the human will, or indicate the damnation of some infant, or that God, for His own glory, fore-ordained a vast majority of the race to everlasting death. It has been my good or bad fortune to speak in public and in private, to a large number of persons hostile to our church, and in nearly all cases I have found their hostility based upon the doctrines indicated above, and in all ways, I have declared to them that the Presbyterian Church had left behind those doctrines, and that her religion was simply Evangelical, and not *par excellence* the religion of despair. In my peculiar ministry a simple silence has not been sufficient. I have, therefore, at many times, declared our denomination to be simply a church of the common Evangelical doctrines.

Besides the formulas of its books, our church has

suffered more than pen can record, from the wild utterances of some of its great names, and from these it has been my frequent duty to try to separate her fair and sweeter present. There were ages when mothers wailed in awful agony over a dead infant, because they had been taught that children "not a span long" were suffering on the hot floor of hell, and each new-born infant was only a "lump of perdition;" and, under the awful lashing of these thoughts, mothers used to baptize their *dead-born* little ones, piteously beseeching God to ante-date the sacred rite. In the midst of this wail of infants damned, Luther himself says, "God pleaseth you when He crowns the unworthy; He ought not to displease you when He damns the innocent."

Against the doctrine of fatalism, as implied in the perfect independence of God's decree as to all human conduct, against the ultra form of human inability, it has been my constant duty, as it seemed, to protect and defend our church from the influence of ideas so repudiated by modern thought. An eminent churchman — perhaps Luther — said, "All things take place by the eternal and invariable will of God, who blasts and shatters in pieces the freedom of the will."

Next to the baneful Calvinistic estimate of the will, comes the overstatement of the idea of salvation by faith all along through the Presbyterian history. Said

Luther, "You see how rich is the Christian. Even if he would, he could not destroy his salvation by any sins, however grievous, unless he refuse to believe." "Be thou a sinner and sin boldly, still more *boldly believe.* From Christ no sin shall separate, though a thousand times a day we should commit fornication and murder." In my ministry I have toiled the harder to unite faith and holiness, because of this dreadful page of history written down against the Calvinistic branches of the Protestant Church.

Next to the injury the Presbyterian Church has sustained from its errors as above mentioned, it has become a source of actual infidelity by its terrific doctrine of hell. Even to the day of Edwards, and since, the pictures of perdition have been such as at first, indeed, to frighten the multitude, but such as afterward to destroy the idea of God. Look where men might, it was perdition to all but his sect, and to look upon other sects in the pains of hell, was to form a part of the happiness of the blessed. The faggot, the rack, and the boiling oil were the resort of potentates, for, if God was so glorying in the torment of heretics just beyond, it was a small matter if the church tormented them slightly on this side the tomb. We need not disguise the fact, my brethren, that the dark side of Calvinism gave birth to infidelity in that age when the church was narrow in its love, broad only in its damnation. But permit me to quote from one who has not been arraigned for bad teaching, but whose words have just been published by the American Tract Society,— Theodore Christlieb. He says: "It was the former century which prepared the way among ourselves for the prevalence of Rationalism. Was it not the petrifaction of Evangelical faith into dry forms of a dead orthodoxy? The sermons of that period were for the most part * * * about Crypto-Calvinists, Syncredists, Synergists, Majorists, Antinomians, Osiandrians, Weigelians, and Arminians. * * * At such a time, when a cold orthodoxy was almost everywhere substituted for living faith, when a slavish adherence to the church's standards was put in place of a free inquiry into the sense of Scripture, and a fresh bondage to the letter was introduced, it became a simple necessity for energetic minds like Lessing to come to an open breach with traditional Protestantism. * * * Rationalism was right in contending for simple morality in opposition to a theoretic orthodoxy." "It must be confessed that the church theology of the last century was chiefly to blame for the general apostasy from the ancient faith which then began. From the middle of the eighteenth century to the end of the first third of the nineteenth, the chief authorities in pulpits and institutions of learning, were promoters of Rationalism. * * * For this spirit, we theologians have only ourselves to thank. We are now reaping what we ourselves have sown."

Such are the words of a profound thinker, who, to his fame as a thinker, adds a parallel fame of piety. Amid some of the unparalleled doctrines of our church arose the intellectual revolt of the present times, and we can only check the progress of the evil by withdrawing the cause. It is an ominous fact, that the Liberal creed which the charges in this case attack, has come chiefly from that land which once lay wholly subject to the severe tenets of the Puritans.

It seems to me the world is now fully ready for an orthodoxy that shall firmly, yet tenderly, preach all of the creed, except its plain errors of dark views of God and man. Not one of you, my brethren, has preached the dark theology of Jonathan Edwards in your whole life. Nothing could induce you to preach it, and yet it is written down in your creed in dreadful plainness. Confess, with me, that our beloved church has slipped away from the religion of despair, and has come unto Mount Sion, into the atmosphere of Jesus, as He was in life and in death, full of love and forgiveness. And yet it is only in the narrow field just pointed out that I have in any way departed from the doctrines of the Presbyterian Church.

One of the most distinguished of our theological teachers in the east has just written: "There is not enough in that indictment to convict one of heresy. All these commotions only point to a time when sectarianism will disappear, and all Christians will meet on the platform of a common faith in one Christ and one Savior, and, fastening all their faith upon Him as a Redeemer, will cast off many of the forms which now perplex them."

Beloved brethren, holding the general creed as rendered by the former New School Theologians, I will, in addition to such a general statement, repeat to you articles of belief, upon which I am willing to meet the educated world, and the skeptical world, and the sinful world, using my words in the Evangelical sense: The inspiration of the Holy Scriptures, the Trinity, the divinity of Christ, the office of Christ as a mediator when grasped by an obedient faith, conversion by God's Spirit, man's natural sinfulness, and the final seoaration of the righteous and wicked.

I have now read before you an outline of my public method and my Christian creed. It is for you to decide whether there is in me orthodox belief sufficient to retain me in your brotherhood. Having confessed everywhere that the value of a single life does not depend upon sectarian relations, but upon Evangelical or Christian relations, I am perfectly willing to cross a boundary which I have often shown to be narrow; but, going from you, if such be your order at last, it is the Evangelical Gospel I shall still preach, unless my mind should pass through undreamed of changes in the future.

From the prosecutor of this case I would not withhold my conviction that he has acted from a sense of duty; therefore, to him and to you all, brethren, I extend good-will, and hope that in a wisdom religious and fraternal, you will be enabled to do what is right in the sight of God.

Yours, with love,

DAVID SWING.

www.ingramcontent.com/pod-product-compliance
Lightning Source LLC
Chambersburg PA
CBHW021214270326
41929CB00010B/1127

* 9 7 8 3 3 3 7 2 4 9 1 1 3 *